MINORITIES IN
THE UNITED STATES

PUBLICATIONS OF THE CENTER FOR MANPOWER POLICY
STUDIES AT THE GEORGE WASHINGTON UNIVERSITY

MINORITIES IN THE UNITED STATES
Sar A. Levitan, William B. Johnston, Robert Taggart

PROGRAMS IN AID OF THE POOR FOR THE 1970s
Sar A. Levitan

ECONOMIC OPPORTUNITY IN THE GHETTO
Sar A. Levitan, Garth L. Mangum, Robert Taggart

SOCIAL EXPERIMENTATION AND MANPOWER
Sar A. Levitan, Robert Taggart

LOW-INCOME HOUSING: A CRITIQUE OF FEDERAL AID
Robert Taggart

EMPLOYMENT AND EARNINGS INADEQUACY
Sar A. Levitan, Robert Taggart

WORK AND WELFARE GO TOGETHER
Sar A. Levitan, Martin Rein, David Marwick

STILL A DREAM: THE CHANGING STATUS OF THE BLACKS
Sar A. Levitan, William B. Johnston, Robert Taggart

THE QUEST FOR A FEDERAL MANPOWER PARTNERSHIP
Sar A. Levitan, Joyce K. Zickler

HUMAN RESOURCES AND LABOR MARKETS
Sar A. Levitan, Garth L. Mangum, Ray Marshall

INDIAN GIVING: THE FEDERAL GOVERNMENT AND NATIVE AMERICANS
Sar A. Levitan, William B. Johnston

OLD WARS REMAIN UNFINISHED: THE VETERANS BENEFIT SYSTEM
Sar A. Levitan, Karen Cleary

MINORITIES IN
THE UNITED STATES

Problems, Progress, and Prospects

By

SAR A. LEVITAN
WILLIAM B. JOHNSTON
ROBERT TAGGART

Public Affairs Press, Washington, D. C.

51869

77-12087

Published by Public Affairs Press
419 New Jersey Avenue, S. E., Washington, D. C. 20003
Printed in the United States of America
Library of Congress Catalog Card No. 75-21685

301.45
LEV

CONTENTS

About the Authors

Sar A. Levitan is Research Professor of Economics and Director of the Center for Manpower Policy Studies at The George Washington University. He is a graduate of the City College of New York, B.S.S. 1937, and Columbia University, Ph.D. 1949.

Robert Taggart is Executive Director of the National Manpower Policy Task Force. He is a graduate of the College of William and Mary, B.A. 1967, and George Washington University, Ph.D. 1973.

William B. Johnston is Research Associate at the Center for Manpower Policy Studies at The George Washington University. He is a graduate of Yale University, B.A. 1967, and presently taking graduate courses at The George Washington University.

PREFACE

The 1960s brought massive changes in the economic, political, and social status of minorities in the United States. Most of these changes represented progress, though some were equivocal and a few may have been steps backward. Now as economic conditions have worsened and the nation's commitment to social progress seems to have wavered, many gains which were applauded only a few years ago are losing support and are deteriorating. There is the ominous prospect of a bitter struggle as minority groups who have been promised a more equal share, and who have perhaps even tasted some of the fruits of greater opportunity, are pushed away from the table as entrenched factions fight for shares of a smaller economic pie.

Whether this slowdown of progress for minorities signals an important change in the nation's social agenda or only a temporary aberration in the long-term pattern of improvement, it is an opportune time to assess how far we have come in the quest for economic and social justice. Indisputably we are far from an equal opportunity society. Indisputably we have made important strides since 1960. Where do we stand? Where do we go from here?

This book seeks partly to answer these questions by organizing, synthesizing, and abstracting the basic factual information concerning the changing status of blacks, Puerto Ricans, Mexican-Americans, and American Indians. Rather than a comprehensive study or a pointed thematic presentation, the volume aims to provide the highlights of the data and to sketch the broad patterns as they are revealed by federally-

1

published statistics and other public and private resource documents.

There is value in the telescoping of the evidence. To some extent the problems come into sharper focus when they are seen in "headline" form without the distractions of a welter of details and disputed interpretations. The comparative problems of different groups are also clearer when they stand side-by-side in a distilled format. Are blacks worse off economically? Are the language problems of Spanish minorities more critical than those of Indians or blacks? How do family patterns among different groups affect their economic and social progress? These questions, of course, cannot be answered definitively, but the basic facts concerning each group can shed considerable light on these issues.

Whatever the value and importance of further and more detailed study, there is a need to ground present concerns on facts rather than rhetoric. Too much of recent argument has revolved around inflated or misleading statistics coupled with long-term projections of temporary trends. Hopefully this study can provide a foundation and perspective to guide policymakers and others toward the continued implementation of a better and an equal opportunity society.

We are indebted to Leo Estrada, A. J. Jaffe, and Zaida Carreras Carleton for the use of unpublished reports they prepared for The Ford Foundation. These reports cover materials that appear in Chapters III and IV.

This volume was prepared under a grant from The Ford Foundation to The George Washington University's Center for Manpower Policy Studies. In accordance with the Foundation's practice, complete responsibility for the preparation of the volume was left to the authors.

Sar A. Levitan
William B. Johnston
Robert Taggart

Washington, D. C.

I

OVERVIEW

Blacks, Mexican-Americans, Puerto Ricans, and Indians together account for between one-seventh and one-sixth of the nation's population. The breakdown in 1973 was as follows:*

	(millions)	Percent of U.S. Population
Total	*32.5*	*15.4*
Blacks	23.7	11.2
Mexican-Americans	6.0	3.0
Puerto Ricans	1.6	.8
Indians	0.9	.4

While there are very substantial variations within and between these groups, they are all disproportionately represented among the deprived, disadvantaged, and disenfranchised by almost every measure of socio-economic status.

Income, Employment, and Educational Deficiencies

The 1970 census statistics, though questionable on some counts, leave no doubt about the gaps in income, employment and education. The mean per capita income of blacks, Mexican-Americans, Puerto Ricans, and Indians in 1969 was less than 54 percent that of all whites. Minorities accounted for more than a third of the poor and nearly two-fifths of all families receiving welfare (and since 1969 these proportions

* Recent census tallies have been criticized for undercounting minorities. The Bureau of the Census itself has estimated that the actual minority group populations may be from 3 to 10 percent greater than the published figures.

3

CHART 1. PER CAPITA INCOME AND POVERTY INCIDENCE, 1969

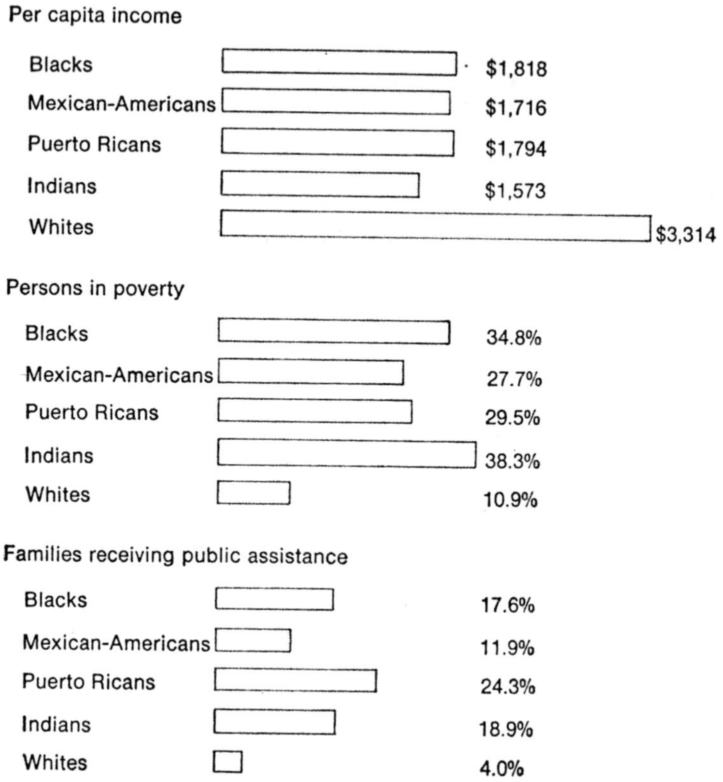

Per capita income

Blacks	$1,818
Mexican-Americans	$1,716
Puerto Ricans	$1,794
Indians	$1,573
Whites	$3,314

Persons in poverty

Blacks	34.8%
Mexican-Americans	27.7%
Puerto Ricans	29.5%
Indians	38.3%
Whites	10.9%

Families receiving public assistance

Blacks	17.6%
Mexican-Americans	11.9%
Puerto Ricans	24.3%
Indians	18.9%
Whites	4.0%

Note: These and other 1970 census data refer to persons identifying themselves as of Mexican and Puerto Rican origin. "Whites" includes most of
these two groups.

have risen). Comparatively, blacks had slightly greater
per capita income, but both Spanish minorities had fewer
persons in poverty. Indians were worst off on both counts
(Chart I).

Employment problems are the major cause of low income.
Black, Mexican-American, Puerto Rican, and Indian workers
are concentrated in low-paying, unstable jobs at the bottom of
the occupational ladder. In 1970, they were twice as likely

as whites to be in service or laboring occupations. Their unemployment rate was almost three-fourths higher than for whites, and they accounted for a fifth of the unemployed, though only an eighth of the labor force. Minority males experience lower labor force participation rates and more frequent work interruptions than whites. Except for Indians, whose status in depressed reservation economies is far worse than that of any other group, blacks suffer the greatest occupational and employment handicaps, with more workers in service and laboring jobs and with higher rates of male unemployment and nonparticipation in the labor force (Table 1).

TABLE 1. LABOR MARKET STATUS, 1970

	Blacks	Mexican-Americans	Puerto Ricans	Indians	Whites
Workers in service and laborer occupations, 1970					
Males	35.5%	33.1%	26.5%	29.4%	14.5%
Females	44.0	31.8	15.7	36.1	18.7
Unemployment, 1970					
Males	6.3	6.1	5.6	11.6	3.6
Females	7.7	8.9	8.7	10.2	6.8
Male labor force participation, 1970	69.8	77.4	76.1	63.4	77.4
Males working full-year, 1969	58.2	59.3	62.1	49.5	68.4

While the relationship between education and economic status varies for different groups, those who are better educated are more likely to find well-paying, stable, and more satisfying jobs. It is critical, therefore, that among persons aged 25 years and over in 1970, 58 percent of whites, but three in ten minority group members had a high school diploma. Minorities accounted for a fifth of those with less than a high school education, but less than one in twenty college graduates. Puerto Ricans and Mexican-Americans

CHART 2. YEARS OF SCHOOL COMPLETED
PERSONS 25 YEARS AND OVER, 1970

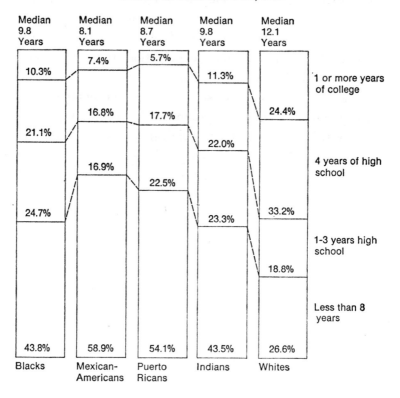

Median 9.8 Years	Median 8.1 Years	Median 8.7 Years	Median 9.8 Years	Median 12.1 Years	
10.3%	7.4%	5.7%	11.3%		1 or more years of college
21.1%	16.8%	17.7%		24.4%	
	16.9%		22.0%		4 years of high school
24.7%		22.5%		33.2%	
			23.3%		1-3 years high school
				18.8%	
					Less than 8 years
43.8%	58.9%	54.1%	43.5%	26.6%	
Blacks	Mexican-Americans	Puerto Ricans	Indians	Whites	

TABLE 2. FAMILY STRUCTURE, 1970

	Blacks	Mexican-Americans	Puerto Ricans	Indians	Whites
Percent children under 18 years living with both parents	57.3%	80.2%	64.1%	68.6%	82.7%
Percent families headed by female	27.4	13.4	24.4	18.4	9.0
Females aged 16 years years and over					
Married with husband present	44.1	58.8	55.0	54.3	62.0
Widowed, divorced, spouse absence	32.5	17.8	25.5	23.5	19.0

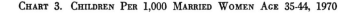

CHART 3. CHILDREN PER 1,000 MARRIED WOMEN AGE 35-44, 1970

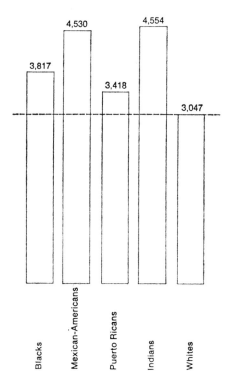

have considerably less education than either blacks or Indians (Chart 2).

Other Compounding Problems

Income, education, and employment deficiencies are compounded by other factors. The limited family incomes of minorities must feed more mouths, and must rise rapidly to merely keep ahead of population growth. In 1970 minority fertility rates for ever-married women aged 35 to 44 were a third higher than whites (Chart 3).

Minority families with children under 18 years had an average of 2.8 children compared with 2.3 for whites. For

every 100 potential breadwinners over age 18 there were
73 younger dependent blacks, 110 Mexican-Americans, 87
Puerto Ricans, and 82 Indians, compared with 50 whites.
Husband-wife families are less prevalent and less stable
among minorities as a whole, and the greater incidence of
female-headed families is a cause of low income. In 1970,
62 percent of minority youths under 18 years were living
with both parents, compared with 83 percent of whites.
Nearly three of ten female family heads were black, Mexican-American, Puerto Rican, or Indian. Minority women
were less likely to be married with a husband present and
substantially more likely to be widowed, divorced, or separated (Table 2).

Compounding the employment and education problems of
minority groups are their geographical concentration and
frequent isolation. Eighty-seven percent of all Mexican-
Americans counted by the 1970 census resided in California,
Texas, Arizona, Colorado, and New Mexico. Almost three-
fourths of all Puerto Ricans lived in New York and New
Jersey, with New York City alone accounting for three-fifths.
Approximately three of every five Indians resided on or near
reservations and 55 percent lived in rural areas (compared
with only a fourth of the total population). Fifty-three percent of blacks lived in the South (in contrast to 28 percent
of whites), and blacks were also more likey to be central
city dwellers; the ten largest cities contained 28 percent of all
blacks but 9 percent of whites. Disaggregation of data by
census tract level reveals that an overwhelming majority of
blacks, Mexican-Americans, Indians, and Puerto Ricans live
in neighborhoods peopled by their own or other minorities.

Disproportionate numbers are also either immigrants or
migrants from rural to urban areas. In 1970 every fifth person of Mexican origin was foreign born and 55 percent of
Puerto Ricans were born outside the continental United

States. Indians are natives, but a third of urban residents were born in a different state, suggesting that a large proportion had moved from the reservation to the city. Two-fifths of all blacks residing in the North and West in 1970 were born in the South, and a large proportion of central city residents came from rural areas.

The impact of cultural differences is difficult to assess, but these are undoubtedly important factors. In 1970 approximately forty percent of Indians reported speaking a mother tongue other than, or in addition to, English. Seven in ten of the Spanish-surname population in the Southwest reported speaking Spanish in their home in 1970. There is no distinct black language, but clearly the argot of the ghetto and the isolated rural South has a different vocabulary and vernacular which can hinder acceptance and adaption in white, middle-class settings. Problems of migration and assimilation are widely shared experiences of minorities.

The Need for a Closer Look

The 1970 and later census data document what is obvious to every thoughtful observer—that despite the changes and improvements of the 1960s, the average black, Mexican-American, Puerto Rican, and Indian substantially lags the average white in income, employment, and education. Moreover, minorities have relatively higher birth rates and more dependents, are isolated from the mainstream and are more likely to be experiencing the difficulties of migration and adjustment to new environments. Without question, the problems of minorities are real, serious, and continuing.

To understand the causes and implications of the changes, it is necessary to go beyond these generalized comparisons. While minorities have much in common, there are extreme variations within and between groups. The black living in a central city ghetto faces a far different set of conditions than the Mexican-American in a Southwest border town or the Indian on an isolated reservation. The recent migrant from Puerto Rico to Harlem may be substantially different from the mainland-born son or daughter of Puerto Rican parents who has moved from New York to other parts of the country.

Even more basically, a statistical snapshot gives no idea of the dynamics of the situation. Are minorities catching up to whites? Are some groups adjusting faster than others? What price are they paying for the adjustments? Both absolute and relative trends in socioeconomic status, as well as causal variables, must be analyzed to answer such questions. Despite the commonalities of minority problems, it is also necessary to examine as best possible the differences in details in order to identify and assess the most desirable policy alternatives.

II

BLACKS

By most measures of income, occupational status, educational attainment and enrollment, health, housing, and political representation, blacks have made substantial progress since 1960. In some cases the gains were both relative and absolute, for example, the doubling of the black share in professional and technical jobs. In other equally important aspects, however, black progress has been outpaced by that of whites. For example, though the number of poor blacks fell significantly, their share of the poor rose from 26 to 32 percent because white poverty decreased more rapidly. In addition, there are indications that some gains recorded by blacks during the 1960s have been eroded in the past few years. The ratio of black to white family income, which had risen from 0.52 in 1960 to a high of 0.61 in 1969, had fallen back to 0.58 by 1973.

This general, if uneven, record of black progress is further marred by evidence that many blacks have not shared in the gains and are apparently worse off in some ways than they were in 1960. At the same time that record numbers of blacks have obtained middle-class jobs and college educations, black rates of violent crime, welfare dependency, and broken families have reached all time highs.

There is little agreement as to whether economic expansion, federal intervention, legal breakthroughs, changing attitudes, black militancy, or other factors have been most responsible for the changes of the past decade. While it would be presumptuous to attempt to resolve these controversies of

11

measurement and meaning, it is possible to outline some of the outstanding developments in black status since 1960.

Income

The income of blacks has risen substantially since 1960. By the most widely reported indicator—family income— blacks more than doubled their income between 1960 and 1973. Adjusted for inflation, the average black family had two-thirds more purchasing power by 1973. These gains considerably improved black status relative to whites, although the dollar gap between whites and blacks increased (Table 3).

TABLE 3. FAMILY INCOME

Year	Blacks	White	Ratio Black to White
1959	$3,047	$ 5,893	0.52
1965	3,886	7,251	0.54
1970	6,279	10,236	0.61
1973	7,269	12,595	0.58

TABLE 4. INCOME BY TYPE OF FAMILY

	1967			1973		
	Black	White	Ratio	Black	White	Ratio
All families	$4,875	$ 8,234	0.59	$ 7,269	$12,595	0.58
Male head	5,737	8,557	0.67	9,549	13,253	0.72
Wife works	7,272	10,196	0.71	12,226	15,654	0.78
Wife does not work	4,662	7,743	0.60	7,148	11,716	0.61
Female head	3,004	4,855	0.62	4,226	6,560	0.64

Black/white family income comparisons are deceptive because black families are more likely to be headed by women, and tend to have greater numbers of dependents than white families. In addition, the income of black husband/wife families is more likely to be supplemented by the earnings of the wife. In 1973, for example, 35 percent of black families were headed by women, compared to 10 percent of whites; the average black family had 1.8 children under 18 years compared to 1.2 for white families; and 53 percent of black wives worked, compared to 44 percent of whites.

A considerable proportion of the disparity between the incomes of black and white families results from the greater numbers of black families without a male breadwinner. Between 1967 and 1973 the ratio of black to white income in husband/wife families, female-headed families, and families in which the wife worked all rose. The increasing proportion of black female-headed families, however, drove the overall ratio down (Table 4).

Similarly, larger numbers of children in black families mean that blacks are even worse off on a per capita basis. In 1973 black income per person was only 56 percent that of whites, and black families had only 43 percent as much income per child as white families.

The importance of black women's contribution to family income highlights the greater relative gains of black female earners compared to black males. From 1960 to 1972 black men increased their real income by 52 percent while black women gained 112 percent. This large increase for women brought their incomes to an average of 96 percent of those of white women by 1972, while the male gains still left them with about 62 percent of average white male earnings. Indeed, black women with some college education enjoyed average earnings equal to or better than their white counterparts.

Despite earning gains relative to whites of same sex, black women were far worse off than men of either race. As a result, the growing number of black women heading families have become a larger proportion of those in poverty. Burdened with more mouths to feed and frequently prevented from working because of child care responsibilities, almost three-fifths of black women heading families were living in poverty in 1972, and these families comprised a fifth of the poverty population.

A large part of the black income gains in the 1960s could be traced to black migration from the South and to the gains of blacks in the South. In the North and West the ratio of black to white family income actually fell between 1959 and 1972, but because blacks were moving from the South (where their relative earnings position, although on the rise, was much worse), the overall average improved. Since the cost of living is higher in the North, however, some of this gain may be illusory.

All income classes of blacks shared in the gains. From 1960 to 1972 the number of families with incomes less than $3,000 (in constant 1972 dollars) fell from 34 to 18 percent, while the proportion making more than $10,000 rose from 13 to 34 percent. In relative terms, blacks in the two bottom fifths of the income spectrum gained more rapidly than either blacks or whites in the higher fifths (Chart 4).

Although the gains were shared by all income and education groups, the relative earnings gains made by better-educated black males were greater than those of men with fewer years of school. Black men with college degrees, narrowed the relative earnings advantage held by whites with similar education by 40 percent, compared with a 17 percent gain by men with less than 8 years of school. Still, in 1969 a large gap remained with black men typically earning about seven-tenths as much as similarly educated white men. A black man with a college degree earned about $400 less than a white male high school graduate, and a black man with 1 to 3 years of college earned $370 less per year than a white high school dropout.

Younger blacks, whose education most nearly approached that of whites, made the greatest relative earnings gains dur-

CHART 4.
INCOME DISTRIBUTION, WHITE AND NONWHITE FAMILIES (1972 DOLLARS)

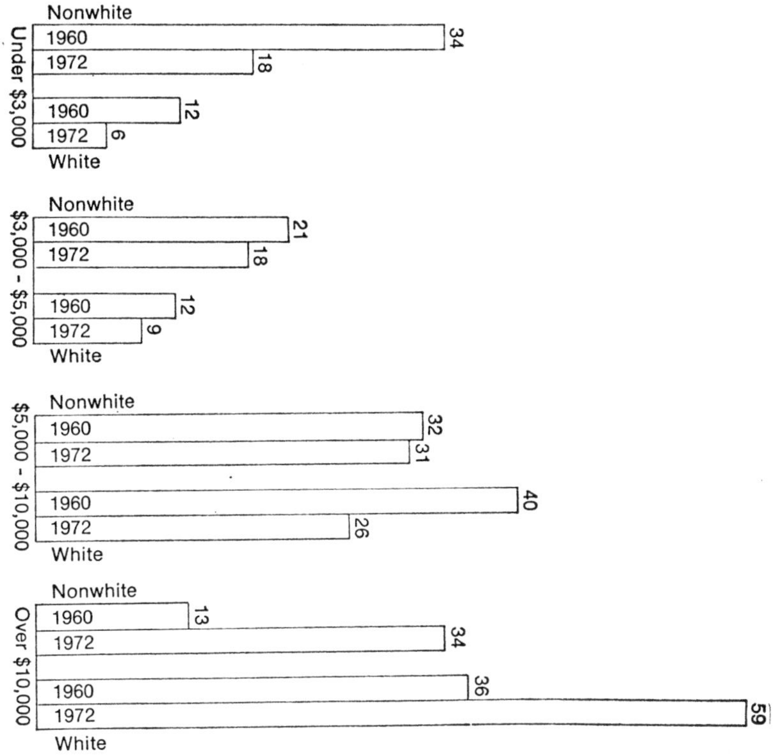

ing the decade, and suffered the least apparent discrimination compared to whites of similar age.)Black men age 25 to 34 with 17 or more years of school earned 84 percent as much as similar whites; for black women of these ages the ratio was 98 percent. By contrast, black male college graduates between the ages of 55 and 64 earned only half as much as similar whites. Hopefully, younger blacks are the leading edge of a process whereby more equal education will lead to more equal opportunity in all age brackets. On the other hand, the progressive effects of discrimination may widen the gap between white and black incomes as these younger workers grow older.

The broad pattern of gains disguises sharp differentials in the sources of the added income. Blacks (and whites) in the lowest income classes are receiving an increasingly large fraction of their incomes from government transfer programs. From 1959 to 1969 the nonearned portion of the income of the nonwhite poor grew from one-quarter to two-fifths. Half of this money was in the form of welfare payments. In the higher income brackets, most of the black gains came from better jobs, not from self employment or returns from capital. In 1972 income from these latter sources represented one-seventh of all white income, but 2 percent of black income.

The meaning of these figures and comparisons is clouded by several factors. For example, the numbers do not take into account regional and residential differentials in the cost of living. Blacks in rural southern areas may be better off earning fewer dollars than their counterparts in northern and urban areas who must pay more for everything. More importantly, the income statistics include only cash income, and fail to list such things as fringe benefits, capital gains, and home ownership, all of which are growing fractions of overall national income. Black gains may be substantially overstated since blacks share less in fringe benefits, capital gains, and the rent savings from home ownership.

On the other hand, the income statistics also do not include government in-kind transfers, such as food stamps, housing, and medical care. Because more of them are poor, blacks are disproportionately represented among recipients of these federally subsidized goods and services. In 1972 blacks received about 22 percent of all in-kind aid, ranging from 47 percent of public housing subsidies to their 6 percent share of Medicare payments (Table 5).

All told, blacks received about $5.5 billion federally supplied goods and services in 1972. Since many of these pro-

TABLE 5. VALUE OF IN-KIND GOODS AND SERVICES, 1972

	Black Share	Dollar Benefit to Blacks (millions)
Total	22%	$5,460
Medicaid	33	2,480
Medicare	6	510
Veterans' health	16	390
Other health	40	330
Food stamps	41	820
Other food programs	25	380
Public housing	47	420
Other housing	30	130

grams were small or nonexistent in 1960, their expansion substantially improved the real income of blacks. Between 1960 and 1972 increases of in-kind aid represented about a 9 percent supplement to reported black income; for whites the benefit amounted to slightly more than 2 percent. For the black poor, in-kind aid was even more important. In 1972 federal transfers of goods and services to poor blacks may have equalled as much as a 50 percent supplement to their cash incomes.

While the balance of these factors is not completely clear, it is obvious that all classes of blacks have gained substantially in real income since 1960. In the middle-income brackets, economic expansion, increasing education, and lowered discriminatory barriers led to better jobs for many blacks, especially black women. Federal assistance, both cash and in-kind, was the key factor in the gains for the black poor.

Optimism over the general pattern of progress toward income equality must be tempered. Proportionally, more blacks than whites remain in poverty and fewer blacks have made it into the upper income classes. Two centuries after the Constitution provided that blacks would be counted as three-fifths of whites for purposes of representation, blacks are still struggling to achieve that income ratio. The steady advances of the 1960s have stagnated or reversed recently with the number of poor blacks actually increasing in the early 1970s. If the economic and legal forces which encouraged the improvements of the 1960s are not renewed, it is problematic whether black income gains will continue.

Employment

Underlying black income advances were, of course, significant improvements in black employment status. Between 1960 and 1973 the proportion of blacks in the three highest paying job classifications—managers and administrators, professional and technical workers, and craftsmen—nearly doubled. During the same period, the proportion in the lowest paying service and laboring jobs dropped by one-third. The occupational status of whites improved less rapidly so that black gains were relative as well as absolute. (Table 6).

The greatest gains were made by black women and younger workers. In 1960, one of three black women was employed as a domestic servant; in 1972, 15 percent held such jobs. The proportion of black women in white collar jobs more

TABLE 6. OCCUPATIONAL DISTRIBUTION

	1960		1973	
	Nonwhite	*White*	*Nonwhite*	*White*
Total	*100.0%*	*100.0%*	*100.0%*	*100.0%*
Professional and technical	4.8	12.1	9.9	14.4
Managerial and administrative	2.6	11.7	4.1	11.0
Sales	1.5	7.0	2.3	6.9
Clerical	7.3	15.7	14.9	17.5
Craftsmen	6.0	13.8	8.9	13.9
Operatives	20.4	17.9	22.2	16.3
Nonfarm laborers	13.7	4.4	9.7	4.6
Private household workers	14.2	1.7	5.7	1.1
Other service workers	17.5	8.2	19.6	10.6
Farm workers	3.2	7.4	2.8	3.7

than doubled during the 1960s from 19 to 40 percent. Black women's gains were especially high in teaching and medical and health specialties as well as in clerical jobs, occupations in which blacks' average earnings generally equalled or excelled those of white women. Younger blacks of both sexes benefited most from better jobs. The proportion of black males under 25 years in professional and technical jobs more than doubled between 1960 and 1972, and the proportion of young black women performing domestic work fell by 85 percent.

Most black gains have been only to the first or second rungs of the higher status occupational categories. For example, in 1969 black men were 6 percent of all male professionals, but only 2 percent of physicians and 1 percent of lawyers and judges, compared to 15 percent of social and recreation workers. In craft jobs, blacks were 7 percent overall, but held less than 5 percent of the top paying jobs such as electricians, foremen, and plumbers, while comprising 30 percent of the next to the lowest-paid occupation, cement and concrete finishers.

The general, if moderate, improvements in occupational status are unfortunately not paralleled by improvements in employment status. Throughout the 1960s and early 1970s, black unemployment rates have consistently remained about double white rates (Chart 5). In 1973 the black rate averaged 8.9 percent, compared to 4.3 for whites. The job problems of black youths have remained especially severe, with more than 30 percent out of work in 1973. In addition to these high annual rates, blacks who become unemployed remain jobless longer and are more likely to suffer recurrent spells of unemployment. These higher rates have consequences in terms of decreased annual earnings, lower average job tenure (with the attendant greater danger of layoffs), and less likelihood of eligibility for pensions and other benefits.

CHART 5. UNEMPLOYMENT RATES, 1960 AND 1973

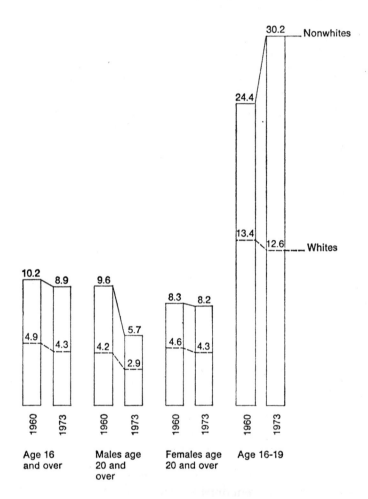

Overall male participation in the labor force declined while the proportion of working women rose. But the rate of decrease among nonwhite males exceeded white declines and nonwhite women experienced a slower increase than whites. (See table on page 21).

While some of this trend was the result of longer educations and earlier retirements, participation rates for black

LABOR FORCE PARTICIPATION RATES

1960	Males	Females
Nonwhite	83.0%	48.2%
White	83.4	36.5
1973		
Nonwhite	73.8	49.1
White	79.5	44.1

men between the ages of 25 and 54 (presumably unaffected by these factors) dropped from 95 to 90 percent, while white rates remained essentially unchanged. It appears that some combination of increased disability coverage, a shortage of well-paying jobs (or an unwillingness to accept low-paying jobs), and the greater availability of income supports may have been responsible for this trend.

The tight labor markets which prevailed through the 1960s were a prime factor contributing to the improvements in black occupational status. The sharp declines in unemployment rates during the late 1960s cut black unemployment by 6 percentage points, compared to a 3 point drop for whites. Continued outmigration from rural farm areas to urban markets contributed to black occupational and earning gains. From 1960 to 1970 the number of blacks employed on farms fell by more than half; many undoubtedly improved their job status after moving to the city. The lowering of black/white educational differences certainly also contributed to the trend toward better jobs by improving blacks' credentials and qualifications. A fourth factor appears to have been a slackening of institutional and individual discrimination. Whether as a result of necessity, morality, or threats of legal actions, blacks gained entrance to many occupations and industries from which they had been excluded.

At least in part this was due to pressure from federal watchdog agencies—the Office of Federal Contract Compliance and the Equal Employment Opportunity Commission.

Initially lacking enforcement teeth and failing to implement extensive affirmative action efforts, these agencies have had more significant impacts in recent years. Following recent settlements in which the EEOC won large back pay and reparations penalities against companies guilty of discrimination, many large corporations have stepped up their affirmative action plans. Since black gains from migration, economic expansion, and improved education may not be repeated in the near future (or at least not at the same rate), the role of federal enforcement machinery may become more crucial if black occupational status is to improve further.

Education

Educational indicators present a mixed picture of progress and stagnation. On one hand, enrollment at every level from pre-school to graduate school has risen for both males and females. Dropout rates have declined, high school and college graduation rates have risen, and the average educational attainment of young blacks has improved, even when compared to white standards. Yet, black rates of high school and college graduation remain well below those of whites, and blacks continue to score less well on reading and mathematics tests, and to fall behind in school.

From 1960 to 1974 median years of school for nonwhites increased from 8.2 to 11.1 years, narrowing the black/white gap from 2.7 to 1.3 years. Most of the gain in the median came from reduced high school dropout rates, with the proportion of graduates in the black population aged 25 years and over nearly doubling in 14 years and reaching 44 percent in 1974. The greatest gains were made by young blacks. By 1973 seven-tenths of blacks aged 20 to 24 had completed high school, and a quarter had spent at least one year in college, compared to 85 and 42 percent for whites. Although black college graduates still represented relatively small fractions of the total black population, their gains during the decade were especially impressive. From 1960 to 1974 the proportion of 25- to 34-year-old blacks with a college degree doubled from 4.1 to 8.1 percent, though this figure was still less than half the 21 percent rate for whites. One further encouraging note was that the ratios of black males and females with longer educations have nearly equalized in recent years, balancing the long-standing pattern of greater educational achievement by black women.

PRE-SCHOOL YEARS

The enrollment of black 3- to 5-year-old children in pre-school programs is an encouraging highlight of the picture of black education. Since 1964, when statistics by race became available, black 3- and 4-year-olds have actually been more likely to be enrolled in school than whites. This is partly due to the larger percentage of black working mothers who have traditionally needed day care as well as educational services for their children. Some of the credit must be allocated to federal programs such as Head Start which have been developed to serve poor children. The fact that black parents of every educational and income class are more likely to enroll children in preschool programs testifies both to the usefulness of pre-primary school programs in opening early education to all segments of society and to the striving of black parents to give their children all the educational advantages possible. Unfortunately, it has not been documented that preschool programs yield lasting educational benefits. Nevertheless, the gains in terms of socialization of children and improved nutritional and health care have made the program popular among black parents and educators.

ELEMENTARY AND SECONDARY SCHOOL

The picture of black education through high school is not as encouraging. From ages 6 to 17 the proportions of blacks enrolled in school have become approximately equal to those of whites for all regions and residence areas of the country. Black high school dropout rates (aged 14 to 20) declined by 27 percent for men and 12 percent for women between 1967 and 1973, compared to drops of 12 percent for white men and 14 percent for white women. These changes still mean that about 18 percent of blacks between the ages of 14 and 24 years have left high school without finishing compared to 11 percent of whites.

Blacks, however, are still more likely to be enrolled in grades below the modal one for their age. More than two-fifths of black males and three in ten females are behind at least one grade in school, approximately double the rates for whites (Table 7). A result of this educational delay is that proportionately twice as many blacks as whites stay on in high school in their 18th and 19th years. Much of the differential in retardation rates can be correlated with the lower education and income, and less stable marital status of black parents. While there is some indication that the comparatively greater rate of retardation in school may have declined from 1960 to 1970, data from more recent years do not suggest much improvement, if any. Moreover, undocumented relaxation of attendance and advancement policies in

TABLE 7. PROPORTION BEHIND IN SCHOOL, ONE GRADE OR MORE, 1973

Male	Age 6	Age 9	Age 12	Age 16
Black	2.6%	27.6%	33.4%	49.8%
White	6.8	17.7	22.7	23.5
Female				
Black	3.4	20.1	25.3	38.0
White	3.8	14.2	15.8	16.6

many schools may have clouded the meaning of the reported improvements in modal enrollment ratios.

The educational difficulties indicated by retardation in school are confirmed by results of reading, mathematics, and entrance tests. Black performance on nationwide tests conducted in 1965 and 1972 averaged about one standard deviation below scores of whites. Again, part of these differences could be explained by differences in the educational and income status of parents.

These data suggest that increases in years of school and percentages enrolled do not guarantee equalized educational opportunity, achievement, or credentials. The continuing difficulty of equalizing black education led to a number of experiments and innovations during the 1960s. Some educators blamed the tests used to measure black students and the school systems which retarded their achievement. This group argued that tests which measure achievement are geared to the standards and couched in the language of the white majority, and that school systems designed for and controlled by whites have slighted black children's needs. These criticisms have led to attempts to develop methods of schooling and testing which are more successful in developing the abilities of blacks. Parents and educators who have sought to obtain more control over their children's educations have sometimes ended practices such as ability tracking and standardized testing, and have developed innovative approaches to education. As yet, however, the educational benefits of these changes have not been proved on any nationwide scale.

A second strategy, based on evidence that the resources expended on black students were unequal to those available to whites, was compensatory funding. The 1960s saw court battles seeking to redistribute state and local resources and national assistance programs which distributed supplemental aid to school districts with disadvantaged students. While these efforts have reduced the inequities in resource distribution, they have not reached a scale of significantly raising the educational resources directed to disadvantaged and black students. The general lack of positive educational results in national tests of students receiving compensatory aid cannot yet be taken as conclusive evidence that compensatory education efforts are ineffective. It would be more precise to conclude that they have not yet been adequately tried.

The third strategy which achieved considerable momentum during the 1960s was integration. On the assumption that the isolation of black students was one of the chief causes of their educational deficiencies, administrators and courts finally began to implement desegregation of the schools in the late 1960s. From 1968 to 1972 the proportion of blacks in predominantly black schools dropped from 68 to 44 percent. Most of this improvement came in the southern and border states, where the proportion in all black schools was cut by 80 percent in four years (Table 8).

TABLE 8. THE CONCENTRATION OF BLACK STUDENTS, 1968 AND 1972

	Total		Southern and Border States		North and West	
	1968	1972	1968	1972	1968	1972
Percent in schools with black majority	76.6	67.2	79.8	57.4	72.4	70.9
Percent in schools 80 percent or more black	68.0	44.5	76.1	36.0	57.4	55.9
Percent in all black schools	39.7	10.9	61.4	11.5	12.3	10.0

This gain was not matched in northern areas, where the *de facto* segregation of many urban districts reached all time highs as a result of continued white flight from neighborhoods and schools. While the legal remedies for continuing and expanding progress toward integration are still being explored, the educational benefits derived from it are under debate. Studies following the educational progress of students in newly desegregated schools have reached conflicting conclusions regarding its effects on learning, though there is some concensus that desegregation can have some small educational benefits if it is accompanied by economic and social integration as well and if school resources are maintained at previous levels.

HIGHER EDUCATION

There have been great gains in the numbers of blacks enrolling and graduating from college. From 1960 to 1973 the number of blacks enrolled in college leaped by nearly 400 percent raising the black proportion of those in college from less than 5 to more than 8 percent. The increases in recent years are especially striking. From 1965 to 1973 the proportion of blacks age 18 to 24 years who were enrolled in college rose by 60 percent, while the white proportion stayed the same. Most of the improvement in college attendance has come from increased high school graduation enlarging the pool of potential college candidates. However, increasing motivation to attend college also helped. From 1960 to 1972 the proportion of 25- to 29-year-old nonwhite high school graduates who obtained college degrees rose from 14 to 17 percent, compared to a rise of from 19 to 34 percent for whites. In 1974, 40 percent of 20- to 21-year-old black high school graduates had finished at least one year of college, compared to 29 percent in 1960.

The likelihood of blacks attending college is most nearly equal to whites when family income stands between $3,000 and $10,000. White youths from more affluent or poorer families have significantly better chances of going to school than blacks in similar circumstances. These figures may provide some explanation for blue collar over-reaction to black advances, i.e., among working class families, blacks have apparently as much chance as whites of going to college.

Less optimistically, blacks may have had less success in college, especially in recent years following increases in enrollment. From 1971 to 1973 while total enrollment remained relative stable, an average of 68 percent of black college freshmen, sophomores and juniors appeared in the tallys for the following year at the next higher grade levels. For whites, the proportion was 81 percent.

Blacks were also more likely to attend smaller, lower-cost schools than whites. On the other hand, the likelihood of being in public and two-year colleges was about the same for blacks as whites, with four-fifths in public schools and 29 percent attending junior colleges. The proportion of blacks in predominantly black colleges has declined as overall black college attendance has risen. The proportion dropped to about one-third in 1972 from 60 percent in 1960.

Blacks are still significantly underrepresented at the nation's largest and most prestigious universities, although they have been penetrating these institutions in greater numbers in recent years. In 1970 blacks were 7 percent of college students nationwide, but 5 percent of those enrolled in Ivy League colleges, 4 percent of those in other elite schools (rated most selective on national admissions standards), 4 percent in military academies, and 3 percent of those on the main campuses of state universities.

Blacks are considerably less likely to go to graduate school than whites, with less than 2 percent holding graduate degrees compared to 4 percent of whites. This pattern has not improved much recently. In 1973 only 3 percent of blacks compared to more than 8 percent of whites under age 34 were enrolled in or had received graduate training. Almost all of this discrepancy could be explained by the lower frequency of college graduation since 44 percent of whites and 49 percent of blacks who completed four years of col-

lege enrolled in advanced studies. A substantial proportion
of black graduate education still takes place at Howard and
Meharry Universities. In 1970 these two accounted for 72
percent of all black dental students and 40 percent of medical students.

As in the case of income and employment, actions by the
federal government have apparently contributed most to
recent black educational gains. At the preschool level, Head
Start has been important in bringing equal educational
opportunity to poor black children. The more massive job
of equalizing elementary and secondary education has not
been as successful, although anti-dropout campaigns may
have had some impacts, and the funds for disadvantaged
students certainly allowed school systems to devote more
attention to the needs of poor blacks. Obviously, federally
mandated integration was also a significant step in many
areas. At the college level, programs encouraging recruit-
ment of black students and providing them with financial
assistance, along with pressure on institutions to raise minority enrollments have certainly had impressive results, at
least in numbers enrolled. The problems of black achievement before and during college indicate that the task of
equalizing black education will not be easy to accomplish,
even if enrollment ratios are matched. Years and perhaps
decades of continuing upgrading efforts will be required to
erase the effects of centuries of education discrimination.

Political and Economic Power

Black participation in the political process and black
representation in positions of authority and control increased appreciably during the decade of the 1960s. Most
notable were the gains in voter registration and in the numbers of black elected officials. In the southern states, the

proportion of voting-age blacks registered to vote rose from 29 percent in 1960 to 64 percent in 1972. Though registration rates in the North and West changed little, these dramatic increases in the South raised the black registration rate for the nation as a whole to nine-tenths the rate for whites.

These gains in voter registration, coupled with the increasing concentration of blacks in urban areas, insured the election of many new black officials:

	U.S. House of Rep.	U.S. Sen.	State Legislators	Mayors	Others
1964	5	0	94	*	*
1968	9	1	172	29	914
1974	15	1	332	127	2,608

*Data not available.

In the 1974 elections this trend continued with blacks adding one new member of Congress, 94 new state legislators, and a substantial number of mayors, city councilmen, county commissioners, and other officials.

These noteworthy gains still leave blacks woefully underrepresented with only 3 percent of U. S. legislators, 3 percent of state legislators, and less than 1 percent of all elected officials nationwide. Moreover, the potential for further improvements is uncertain. Despite a few notable exceptions, most of the blacks elected to political offices have been from predominately black areas. In 1974, 15 of the 16 candidates who were elected to Congress came from districts in which blacks made up at least 42 percent of the population. The apparent requirement of a near majority of voters may limit further progress in increasing the number of black office-holders. By the start of the 93rd Congress, elected in 1972, 11 of the 14 districts in which blacks were as much as 45 percent of the population already had black congressmen. It is unlikely that new gains in black voter registration can do much to provide blacks with the near majorities necessary to elect blacks to office. Moreover, the proportion of blacks exercising their right to vote has been declining more than that of whites in recent years, lowering the black share of votes cast.

There are other clouds on the horizon. The movement toward metropolitan-wide planning in government may be necessary for the long-run viability of metropolitan governments, but it dilutes black voting strength and leverage in policy formation. Revenue sharing—shifting control of the pursestrings from the federal government to state and local officeholders—may compound the problem since few local jurisdictions have shown as much concern and awareness of black needs as federal officials.

The number of black officials in elected offices may still increase during the next few years as the worst cases of underrepresentation of blacks fall to concerted organizational and promotional efforts. But it appears likely that the culmination of this process may leave blacks still significantly underrepresented if blacks living in integrated areas are unable to elect black officials.

Political representation is only one source of power. Managers and officials throughout the public and private sectors make decisions which control and effect other people's lives. Among most of these groups of decisionmakers, black representation has grown rapidly in the last decade or so, but blacks still make up small fractions of individuals with substantial authority (Table 9).

For example, from 1962 to 1972 the number of blacks in the top six slots in the federal bureaucracy (1974 salary above $18,463) grew by almost 8,000 or 600 percent. Yet in 1972 blacks still represented only 3 percent of officials in these positions of authority. From 1960 to 1970 the proportion of blacks among wage and salary managers and

TABLE 9. BLACK REPRESENTATION AMONG
MANAGERS AND DECISION MAKERS, 1972

	Percent Black
Governmnt officials (GS-12 and above)	2.9%
Government officials (GS-16 and above)	1.9
Military officers (0-3 and above)	2.2
Military officers (0-6 and above)	0.9
Federal police	7.5
Local police	7.0
State police	2.3
Lawyers	1.3
Corporate lawyers	0.6
State and local judges	2.3
Private sector managers, wage and salary	1.7
Local union officials	5.7

officials rose by 50 percent. Yet in the private sector the black proportion had not yet reached 2 percent. In the military, the number of blacks with the rank of captain (Army) or higher more than tripled in a decade, yet blacks were only 2.2 percent of such officers in 1972.

Apparently also, most black managerial gains to date have been into distinctly lower echelon positions. In the federal bureaucracy and in the military, for example, the proportion of blacks dwindles steadily as the rank rises. Two percent of "supergraders" (1974 salary $34,607 to $36,000) and less than 1 percent of generals are black. Another indicator may be salary levels. Among all managers and administrators in 1970, 5 percent of those earning less than $6,000 annually were black; when salary levels reached $15,000 and over, only 0.7 percent were black.

Overall, the record of black penetration into managerial positions is considerably better in the public than in the private sector. Among salaried managers and officials, nonwhites increased their proportionate representation among government managers from 2.8 to 6.2 percent, compared to a rise from 1.5 to 2.0 percent in the private sector. In part these results may be attributed to the greater initiatives for affirmative action in government. Aside from token hiring, some of the gain clearly reflects a greater representation of blacks in the management and control of social welfare programs developed during the 1960s. While "maximum feasible participation" may have been more slogan than fact, blacks had an unprecedented share of the managerial positions in community action agencies, manpower training programs, welfare delivery systems, and other social welfare programs. Whatever the balance of costs and benefits of these efforts, the rise of substantial numbers of blacks and other minorities into the managerial ranks must be counted as a significant accomplishment.   *77- /2081*

In the particularly crucial areas of law enforcement and the judicial system, blacks are still woefully underrepresented. Nationwide, blacks are 7 percent of all police, ranging from 8 percent of federal agents to 3 percent of state patrolmen. But despite the affirmative action efforts made in the wake of the riots of the 1960s, underrepresentation in large cities remains severe. In 1972 no large city in the nation had as much as three-fifths the number of black policemen as black representation in the population would require, and most had police forces two or three times as white as their populations. Among lawyers and judges, the proportions are even smaller, with blacks representing only 2 percent of state and local judges. Despite some considerable increases in these proportions during the past several years, blacks are still most often arrested, tried, and sentenced by whites.

Elected, appointed, or bureaucratic offices are the most visible positions of power. Another source of great, if often unseen power, is wealth. Blacks control only a minute share of the nation's income-producing and business assets, and thus have little of this leverage. In 1972 reported black income from capital was only one percent of all such receipts,

a proportion which had not increased in five years. Blacks were less than 2 percent of families with assets greater than $25,000. Most crucially, blacks owned or operated a miniscule fraction of the nation's business. In 1972 blacks owned about 195,000 businesses, or fewer than 2.5 percent of the total with the great majority employing an average of less than one person per firm in addition to the owner. With gross receipts of about $7.2 billion, these firms accounted for less than one percent of the receipts of all firms in 1972.

These figures represent some gains since 1969 when the last census of minority businesses was taken, but it is probable that many of the improvemnts noted in 1972 have been reversed during the recent business downturn. Of all black firms with gross receipts of greater than $5 million in 1973, almost half were construction contractors or automobile dealerships, the hardest hit sectors during the present recession. It is doubtful, therefore, that the widely applauded black entrance into business in recent years has yet realized any substantial change in the second class status of blacks in the business sector.

"Black power" remains more a slogan than a reality. The rapid improvements in black representation among elected officeholders, bureaucratic and appointed officials, and business managers and owners are cause for limited optimism. Blacks have been elected to offices in areas where they comprise near majorities of voters, and they have penetrated in some numbers into middle ranks of managerial control. While these gains are more than token achievements, it is uncertain whether they can be followed by continuing rapid improvements. Lacking a firm base in the business sector and forced to achieve near majorities in order to exert their political leverage, the development of true black economic and political power will probably be a more difficult achievement than the gains of the past decade might indicate.

Coalitions with other minorities as well as white groups sharing similar interests may change the situation, however, and enhance the political position of blacks.

Family Status

The mixed gains in education, employment, and income have been accompanied by several negative developments, one of the most important of which was the deterioration of the black family. The emotional debates generated by Daniel Moynihan's *Report on the Negro Family* have obscured and often prohibited reasonable discussion and analysis of changing family status. Writing in 1965, Moynihan noted the pattern of declining family stability, presented evidence of the greater difficulty experienced by children from broken homes, and concluded that the decay of black society stemmed from the deterioration of the black family. While there is still no consensus concerning the ultimate impacts or meaning of the changes in family structure, the trends reported by Moynihan have become more pronounced since he wrote. While the majority of black families still conform to the husband/wife standard by which family stability is typically judged, there are growing differences between black and white family patterns.

Blacks tend to marry later and have less stable marriages than whites. Thirty-one percent of black women age 20 to 34 were single in 1973, compared to 19 percent of whites. Although later marriage of blacks eventually equalizes the ever-married rates between the races (nearly 19 of 20 of both races eventually marry), higher rates of divorce, separation, abandonment, and widowhood leave more black women without husbands. For women over age 18 in 1973, two-thirds as many blacks as whites were married with a husband in the home:

	Black	*White*
Married, husband present	43.2%	66.6%
Single	20.2	13.1
Husband absent, divorced, widowed	20.4	7.0
Widowed	16.1	13.3

In the primary childbearing years between 25 and 34, for example, only 51 percent of black women were living with husband compared to 82 percent of whites. More distressing, black marital dissolution has been increasing steadily, with rates for divorce, separation, and nonmarriage going up faster than those of whites.

The decline of stable marriage and continued high rates of illegitimacy have resulted in a growing proportion of black families headed by women. In 1974, more than a third of families had female heads, up from a fifth in 1960 (Chart 6). During the same period, the rate for whites rose hardly at all. Of the net additions to the numbers of black families since 1965, an astonishing seven of ten were female-headed.

One consequence of these changes in family status is than an increasing proportion of black children are growing up in homes without both parents. In 1960 three-fourths of nonwhite children were in husband/wife families compared to 92 percent of whites. By 1973 the black rate was down to 56 percent compared to 89 percent for whites.

On the positive side, birth rates for all types of families, both black and white, have been declining. From 1965 to 1973 the average number of children born per woman aged 15 to 44 dropped from 2.7 to 1.6 for blacks, compared to a drop from 1.7 to 1.5 for whites. Most of this decline occurred among younger women, paralleling the decline in marriages in this age group. Also, the greatest drop occurred among low-income nonwhite women, among whom birth

CHART 6. PROPORTION FAMILIES HEADED BY WOMEN, 1960-1974

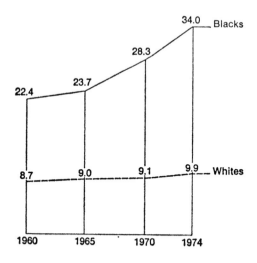

rates fell by 26 percent between the early and late 1960s compared to a drop of only 3 percent among more affluent women. Yet, the relative declines still leave the average black family with more mouths to feed than white families. In 1972 black families averaged 2.6 children per family compared to 2.1 for whites.

Because birth rates for married women fell more rapidly than those for unmarried women, the proportion of black births which were illegitimate rose during the decade. From 1960 to 1971 the illegitimacy rate for nonwhites fell slightly, but legitimate birth rates fell faster, so that the proportion of black children born out of wedlock rose dramatically from

	Legitimate (per 1,000 married women)		Illegitimate (per 1,000 unmarried women)	
	Nonwhite	White	Nonwhite	White
1960	NA	NA	98.3	9.2
1965	186.0	131.3	72.3	11.7
1968	155.9	119.9	68.9	13.1
1971	147.8	116.9	74.1	12.7

22 percent in 1960 to 41 percent in 1971. (See table on p. 37).

Among teenagers—who account for 30 percent of all non-white births two-thirds of all births were illegitimate during 1971 compared to 17 percent among whites.

There are apparently important differences in the acceptability and treatment of illegitimate children among blacks and whites. First, whites appear to be more likely to legitimize their children by "shotgun" marriages. Thirty-four percent of children born to white teenagers come within eight months of marriage compared to 26 percent of those of non-whites. Secondly, an estimated two-thirds of white illegitimate children are given up for adoption or foster care, compared to only 7 percent of blacks. The figures suggest that illegitimacy among blacks is a more socially acceptable pattern and that black families are more likely to accept responsibilities to care for these children.

The reasons for these different marital and family patterns are uncertain as well as controversial. Surveys indicate that blacks tend to have more children because they want more and because they have more unplanned or unwanted births. Black women are less aware of and less often employ various birth control methods, and fewer of them find abortion an acceptable (or available) method of terminating pregnancy. Some surveys also report sexual contact tends to occur at earlier ages for black women.

Speculation as to the reasons for successful marriages have pointed to better education and higher income as key factors, although adjustment for these factors still does not completely explain black/white differences in marital status. Moreover, improvements in education and income over the decade were accompanied by deterioration in family status. The frequently cited reason for changes of recent years has been the impact of welfare support. Blacks, it is argued,

have been encouraged, directly or indirectly, to break up or
not to form families in order to maximize income since
public assistance is primarily available to mothers with
dependent children. While it is not possible to show causal
relationships, the close correlation of the increase in the
number of female-headed families and the number of welfare
recipients argues that public assistance programs have had
a negative impact on black families.

Whatever the causes, the trends toward declining marital
stability, increasing numbers of female-headed families and
more illegitimate and otherwise fatherless children, are disturbing. While the suspected links between these patterns and
crime, educational difficulties, or other problems are not well
established, the consequences in terms of poverty and dependency are unequivocal and negative. Blacks growing up
in such home environments are significantly worse off economically. In 1972 more than half of all black female headed
families were poor, and these families comprised two-thirds
of the black poor. Fifty-five percent of poor, black female
headed families received more than half of their income
from welfare.

Welfare Dependency

Besides contributing to instability in the black family,
the increasing number of blacks on welfare portends long run
social problems for society as a whole. In 1973, 1.4 million black families received welfare payments constituting
46 percent of all families on public assistance. Within a
dozen years the proportion of black families on welfare
rose from 9 to 27 percent. By contrast, less than three percent of white families were on welfare. Since black families on welfare tend to have more children than other black
families, the proportion of children on welfare was even

higher. Two-fifths of black children under 18 years in 1973 were growing up in homes dependent on federal assistance.

This staggering increase in dependency is partly explained by the increase in the proportion of blacks among the poor— from 25 percent in 1960 to 32 percent in 1972. Other factors which may have increased the number of blacks on welfare are the easing of the "man in the house" rule, larger income disregards, and the relaxation of residence requirements. Greater tolerance or sympathy from welfare case workers may also have played a part. In 1973, 79 percent of welfare applications were approved, compared to 54 percent a dozen years earlier.

The decisions of black families to seek welfare were undoubtedly influenced by the rising level of payments. During the decade of the 1960s, welfare benefits rose more rapidly than average earnings. Compared to the salaries available to poor, uneducated women with child care responsibilities, the welfare option became increasingly attractive. In addition, the multiple benefits sometimes available to welfare mothers frequently created "notch" problems whereby full-time employment could lead to a drop in real income. As a result, many families may have stayed longer on welfare; two of every five black families had been receiving assistance for three years or longer in 1971 compared to one-fourth of white families.

By far the most important factor, however, was the rise in the proportion of black families headed by women. Between 1967 and 1973 the number of black families headed by women rose by 684,000, closely paralleling the 744,000 additional black mothers on welfare. At the same time that the number of potential recipients was growing, the proportion of eligibles receiving benefits was also on the rise. In 1960, 21 percent of poor black families received welfare; by 1972 the proportion had reached 55 percent. Apparently, en-

couraged by community action groups, the National Welfare
Rights Organization, and a generally increasing awareness
of the availability of benefits, welfare was becoming more
acceptable to many families.

While there are obvious benefits to black families and
children from the added public assistance income, the de-
bated impacts on family formation may considerably offset
these gains. Direct causal relationships, of course, are uncertain. But it appears that family deterioration has been
promoted by the availability of welfare. In 1971 three-
fourths of black families on welfare reported the husband
absent due to divorce or separation or other reasons, compared to two-fifths of whites. Half of black welfare mothers
reported not knowing where the father resided, compared
with 30 percent among whites. And, roughly half of all
black children receiving assistance were illegitimate compared to less than a fifth of whites. As difficult as it may be to
disentangle cause and effect, it is plausible that a welfare
system which rewards broken families with extra income may
have accelerated family break up.

Polarization in Housing

In terms of size, comfort, and amenities, blacks measurably
improved their housing status during the 1960s. The proportion of blacks residing in "substandard" units according
to the census fell by 45 percent between 1960 and 1968, or
from 44 to 24 percent of all black households. Overcrowding
also declined; 19 percent of nonwhites were in households
with more than one person per room in 1970, down from 28
percent in 1960. Some of these black gains may be attributed
to the movement to the city from rural areas. But there were
improvements in housing standards in both metropolitan and
nonmetropolitan areas during the decade.

These gains by blacks were outstripped, however, by improvements in white housing status, so that those in substandard and overcrowded housing were increasingly likely to be black. In 1970 nonwhites were four times as likely to be in substandard units as whites and three times as likely to be overcrowded, proportions equal to or above those prevailing a decade earlier. Not only lower incomes but housing discrimination were important factors in the continuing gap between black and white housing. Often trapped in delapidated ghettos, blacks were more likely to be living in substandard housing, even when their incomes equalled those of whites. In 1970 only 11 percent of whites with incomes under $5,000 lacked adequate plumbing compared to 25 percent of blacks in his bracket.

The majority of blacks not living in substandard housing also made gains during the decade. The proportion of black homes having appliances such as washers, dryers, freezers, air conditioners, and televisions climbed rapidly during the decade, although in most cases proportionately more whites than blacks made these gains. For example, 98 percent of black families lacked a clothes dryer in 1960 compared to 88 percent in 1970; for whites the proportions were 83 and 58 percent. Blacks also were slightly more likely to own their own homes in 1970 than a decade earlier. Still, the 42 percent of black families in owner occupied homes in 1970 was only two-thirds of the white proportion of 63 percent. Moreover, the value of black homes averaged only two-thirds that of whites.

Blacks trapped in the central cities with high crime rates, low quality municipal services, decaying educational systems, and all the other ills of ghetto environments may value location more than comforts and amenities in the home. Despite the open housing efforts of the 1960s, residential segregation increased during the past decade. In part this was due to choice. From 1960 to 1970, 1.3 million blacks left southern rural areas and more than 2 million blacks migrated to urban areas in the North and West. Since most of the movement of blacks was into the central cities rather than the suburbs, these areas became increasingly black. In 1970 four-fifths of blacks living in the northcentral and northeastern part of the U. S. lived in central cities. Blacks were more than a fifth of the residents of central cities, but only 5 percent of those in the suburbs.

Compounding black migration was the impact of "white flight." From 1960 to 1970, a net of approximately 6 million whites left the central cities for the suburbs and for nonmetropolitan areas. When these data are disaggregated, the extent of racial polarization becomes even more evident. Census samples from 20 large cities revealed that from 1960 to 1970 the proportion of blacks living in census tracts with more than 75 percent black grew from 36 to 50 percent, while mixed neighborhoods in which blacks were 25 percent or less declined from 25 to 16 percent. City by city analysis of this pattern indicated that white flight seemed to be triggered when the proportion of blacks in the neighborhood reached 15 to 20 percent.

Surveys since 1970 suggest that these patterns are continuing, Although the net influx of blacks from the South and into central cities has declined and even reversed since 1970, a net of 5.6 million whites (almost equal to the total for the previous decade) left the central cities between 1970 and 1974. No corresponding migration by blacks to the suburbs was evident, with blacks making up only 4 percent of those migrating to areas outside the urban core.

These statistics are disturbing. Despite federally legislated fair housing standards and despite reports from attitude surveys indicating that whites are becoming less opposed to integrated housing, segregation is steadily increasing. Not only does this complicate efforts to equalize education and occupational opportunities, but the lack of contact between the races also breeds ignorance, superstition, and alienation. In addition, black upward mobility may also be hindered, as middle class blacks are unable to isolate their children from the negative social and physical impacts of ghetto environments.

Whatever the balance of gains and losses, black housing status remains a critical problem. A fourth of blacks still live in homes which are delapidated or lacking in adequate plumbing. A fifth live with more than one person per room. Blacks at all income levels are less likely to own their own homes and these homes are older, less valauble, and have fewer amenities than those of whites. Most seriously, the neighborhoods in which blacks are increasingly concentrated are all-black ghettos in which crime, poor city services, and social isolation produce environments of fear and despair.

Lawlessness

Perhaps the most disturbing trend of the 1960s was the dramatic increase in the rates of violent crime by blacks. Between 1964 and 1972 arrest rates of blacks for violent crime increased by 73 percent compared to a 64 percent rise among whites. In 1972, blacks were from 7 to 17 times more likely to be arrested for violent crimes as whites, and blacks were more than half of those arrested for such crimes (Table 10).

TABLE 10. URBAN ARREST RATES PER 1,000 POPULATION, 1972

	White	Black	Black Percent Total
Murder and nonnegligent manslaughter	4	56	60%
Rape	6	58	49
Robbery	25	414	67
Aggravated assault	58	416	45

Although most violent crimes are committed against victims of the same race, far more whites are victimized by violent black crimes than vice versa. A 1967 study of 17 cities found that 10.5 percent of rapes involved black offenders and white victims, compared to 0.3 percent with the races reversed; similarly, 46.7 percent of armed robberies were committed by blacks against whites, compared to 1.7 percent of whites robbing blacks.

Obviously, the higher incidence of violent crime among blacks is partly explained by the age and income status of blacks. Violent crimes are much more likely among the young and poor; the black population includes, of course, greater numbers of poor youths. Yet in each age and income bracket violent crime rates are substantially higher among blacks. For example, in 1972 among persons under age 18, the black arrest rate for violent crimes was 13 times higher than that for whites. Young blacks comprised one-eighth of the youth population and two-fifths of youths in poverty but accounted for five-eighths of all violent crimes committed by youths. Moreover, if age and income were the controlling factors, it would be impossible to explain why black crime rates exploded during a period of relatively stable age distributions and rising incomes. Ghetto living environments obviously play some part. But this, again, leaves a large portion of black crimes unexplained. For example, Puerto Ricans are 15 percent of the population in New York City compared to 20 percent blacks. The socio-economic status, ghetto living environments, and youthful population of the two groups are comparable. Yet in 1972 blacks accounted for 63 percent of those arrested for violent crimes in New York while Hispanics were 15 percent.

Evidently, cultural factors peculiar to blacks are involved, and these factors must have become more important in recent years. During the 1960s, as blacks were freed of longstanding inhibitions against aggressiveness towards whites, growing numbers of young blacks evidently began to act out violent fantasies, especially when the risks of, and penalties for, apprehension were relatively small. Blacks with little stake in society, who might encounter little stigma or even approbation from their peers apparently began to feel that violent crime was one of the alternatives to hustling, low-paid employment, or joblessness.

Speculation on the causes of these patterns and trends involves many uncertainties and guesses, but the unquestioned fact is that black crime-proneness increased considerably during a decade of progress on other fronts. Whether this is a temporary aberration or long-term trend is still to be determined, but for the present black crime remains a most serious problem.

The Clouded Outlook

Drawing trend lines from this welter of data is as much speculation as science, and striking a balance between the positive and negative developments depends mostly on the observer's predispositions. Nevertheless, the experience of the 1960s and the new developments of the early 1970s suggest that black progress on most front will not be as easily won in the future as it was in the past.

The most recent data for black employment, education, and income suggest that even before the recent economic downturn there was a distinct leveling off of earlier progress. Relative black income gains did not recover with the economy in 1972 and 1973, but continued downward. Relative black unemployment rates which had edged down to levels about 80 percent above white rates in 1970 and 1971 returned to ratios more than double the rising white rates. At the same time, nonparticipation in the labor force among black men of prime working ages continued to drop, absolutely and relative to whites.

The number of blacks in college fell from 1972 to 1973 (although this may be a statistical aberration) and the drop-out rates of college enrollees during the last several years indicate that not all the newly enrolled black college students have sufficient background or support to finish school. At the high school level, there were few reports of narrowing achievement gaps, and in 1973 black dropout rates among those age 14 to 19 reversed their earlier downtrend and were up slightly. While none of these developments was a marked or dramatic turnaround, and most were small enough to be statistical variations, they did give cause for concern.

As the progress slowed on those fronts where it had been greatest during the 1960s, the negative trends continued. Racial isolation as a result of white flight was apparently accelerated, with as many whites leaving the central cities during the first four years of the 1970s as left during the decade of the 1960s. Stable black families were still in decline, with a majority of the new families formed being headed by women and more than half of all black children in homes without both parents. Although overall rates were down, the proportion of children born illegitimately was still climbing. And black crime rates continued to rise steadily, reaching all time highs.

These discouraging developments indicate first that there is little momentum of improvement and that hard won gains can be easily lost if efforts are not sustained. Moreover, they suggest that the debate concerning the ascendency of the black middle class is not an idle numbers game. Presumably if some significant majority of blacks with middle class incomes and middle class values had truly achieved predominance in the black community, then some self-sustaining progress should have been generated and crime, dependency, and family breakup should have abated. This was obviously not the case. The indications that progress has bypassed many blacks whose socio-economic status has worsened, and the suggestions that progress may have slowed for all blacks, argue that we are many years away from a circumstance in which the black community is in the mainstream of American society—with a strong middle class providing the income, power, and values which are necessary if blacks are to reach equal status.

Several factors suggest that black prospects in the future are less encouraging. First, economic woes currently facing the country will certainly hurt blacks worse than whites. Those with the most recent jobs will be the first laid off, those with the lowest incomes will be the most hurt by price rises.

Second, the leverage of the government to effect or force change has been weakened. Government support of social welfare programs is at least temporarily waning, and the rule changes which once promised to legislate and adjudicate black equality have encountered stubborn resistance as the rights of others were affected. Busing to achieve integration has aroused powerful opposition; affirmative action in hiring has encountered union resistance; preferential admissions policies in education and politics have been challenged. Where changes have been made, the results have not always been significant or sustained. For example, where integration has been implemented, it has not brought the dramatic achievement gains originally hoped for. And, while large employers have hurried to bring their hiring practices into nondiscriminatory compliance and have sought to hire some blacks at all levels of employment to counter charges of bias, there is not yet any evidence that these one-time gains will lead to sustained improvements.

The recent past, then, is obviously no cause for rejoicing.

(Not only are the gaps between black and white decades wide
in many cases, the pace of improvements is slow or nonexistent. Only renewed emphasis and long-term support
by government and a so far undetected willingness by a
majority of whites to accept racial equality can bring continued black gains. Even then, the rate of progress is not
likely to equal that experienced during the 1960s.)

III

MEXICAN-AMERICANS

Mexican-Americans are the "hidden" minority. Ranking second in population to blacks, numbering four times Puerto Ricans and eight times Indians, "Chicanos" and their needs have never received commensurate visibility and attention. Stereotypes and misconceptions exist about all minorities, but they are especially pervasive and perverse for Mexican-Americans, who are caricatured as migrant farm workers whose poverty is exacerbated by too many children. The facts are in marked contrast: rural migrant workers account for only a small proportion of all Mexican-Americans, and the closeknit Chicano family has significantly declined in size.

One reason why Mexican-Americans remain "hidden" and misunderstood is the dearth of reliable information. There is no general agreement even on numbers. In March 1974, 6.5 million persons identified their origin or descent as being Mexican-American, Chicano, Mexican, or Mexicano, but such nationwide data on self-identified origin only date from 1970 when only 4.5 million were counted largely because of a less inclusive definition (Table 11). The 1970 and previous censuses tabulated information for persons of Spanish-surname in the southwestern states of California, Texas, Colorado, New Mexico, and Arizona. Roughly a fourth of these Spanish-surnamed were not of Mexican origin, and one in eight Mexican-Americans reside outside the Southwest, so that trend analysis based on surname data can be misleading.

TABLE 11. ALTERNATIVE COUNTS OF MEXICAN-AMERICANS, 1970 AND 1973

	1970 Census			Current Population Survey	
	Spanish-Surname	Spanish Origin	Mexican Origin	Spanish Origin	Mexican Origin
Total U.S.	....	9,073	4,532	10,577	6,293
Southwest	4,668	5,009	3,939	6,273	....

* The different terms reflect individual preferences but this report uses Mexican-American and Chicano interchangeably.

Outside official census sources, there is a limited supply of information about many vital socioeconomic character-istics and trends. Compared to blacks, this literature is meager. In many respects, therefore, Mexican-Americans remain "hidden," and only the most obvious characteristics can be stated with any accuracy.

Income

One fact which is unequivocally documented is the depri-vation of Mexican-Americans. In 1973 the median income of families with a head of Mexican origin was $7,900, or 71 percent the median for all U.S. families. But while the latter averaged 3.6 members, there were 4.4 persons per Mexican-American family. With more mouths to feed, 24 percent of Chicano families, containing a third of all Chicano children, were poor in 1972. Mexican-American economic status was marginally better than blacks, Puerto Ricans, or Indians, but significantly trailed the white population.

Mexican-Americans have made substantial progress in income during the 1960s, though they have closed the gaps relative to whites only modestly. From 1959 to 1969 the median income of Spanish surname males in the Southwest rose by almost three-fourths, increasing from 70 to 75 per-cent of the national male median. The median income of

Chicano females rose four-fifths, or from 87 to 90 percent of national female medians:

	Income of Persons	
	1959	1969
Spanish-surname in Southwest		
Males	$2,804	$4,839
Females	1,065	1,929

The greatest relative improvements were experienced by the younger Chicanos. Possibly because they start work earlier than other whites and more Chicanos work full time, the median income of 20- and 24-year-old males rose between 1959 and 1969 from 0.93 to 1.17 of the Anglo median in the Southwest. For 25- to 34-year-olds the ratio rose from 0.79 to 0.83. In contrast, the median income of 35- to 44-year-old Chicano males fell from 0.77 to 0.73 percent of the Anglo median.

Apparently, there has been some stagnation or reversal in the last few years. The median income of Mexican-origin males nationwide remained at 74 percent of the white median between 1969 and 1973, while for females it fell from 89 to 85 percent. Since the start of the 1960s, then, the relative gains were modest for Chicano males and nonexistent for females, as far as can be judged from limited recent data:

	Income of Persons	
	1969	1973
Mexican origin in U.S.		
Males	$4,735	$5,978
Females	1,892	2,388

The concommitants of low income are also evident. A study in San Antonio indicated that the Chicano male's life expectancy was 2.6 years less than that of Anglos; with a differential among females of 6.6 years. A study of Colorado's Spanish-surnamed citizens found that in 1960 the average age at death for those who had lived more than one year was 57, compared with 67 for the state as a whole; infant mortality rates were also twice as high among Chicanos. A California study found lower rates of illness and chronic disease, but higher rates of disability among Mexican-Americans.

Housing is also a problem, with three in ten Spanish-surname households in the Southwest overcrowded in 1970 compared with 18 percent of black and 8 percent of all households nationwide. In 1960 three in ten Chicano homes were substandard. Though the incidence has undoubtedly declined with increased urbanization, the proportion now living in delapidated homes with inadequate facilities remains several times the national average.

Employment

Mexican-Americans are work-oriented, and their income problems are not the result of dependency or labor force withdrawal. In 1970 roughly one in nine Chicano families received public assistance, compared with one in four Puerto Rican, one in five Indian, one in six black families, and about one in thirty white families not included in the above groups. Because labor force participation rates for males equalled, and those of females exceeded, national averages, and extended families were more prevalent, 50 percent of Mexican-American families had two or more earners in 1970, compared with 35 percent of Puerto Rican and black families and 43 percent of all families.

The problem is that Chicano workers end up in low-paying jobs. In 1970 two-thirds of southwestern Chicano males and three in ten females were craftsmen, operatives, or laborers compared with only 44 and 11 percent respectively, of Anglos, or 60 and 16 percent of black men and women in this area (Table 12).

TABLE 12. OCCUPATIONAL DISTRIBUTION OF
SOUTHWESTERN CHICANOS AND ANGLOS, 1970

	Males		Females	
	Spanish Surname	Other White	Spanish Surname	Other White
Professional, technical and managerial	12%	33%	10%	24%
Sales and clerical	11	16	10	24
Service	11	7	26	17
Craftsmen and operatives	46	36	24	9
Laborers	21	8	6	2

Overrepresented in the lowest rungs in each occupational class as well as in the lowest paying establishments within industries, Chicanos earn less. In 1970 earnings of Spanish-surname males were 74 percent of the Anglo median in California and 59 percent in Texas. Chicano male professionals earned 17 percent less than Anglos in California and 30 percent less in Texas, operatives earned 7 and 28 percent less respectively; similar differentials occur in all broad occupational categories except laborers.

While still substantial, these occupational and earnings differentials narrowed during the 1960s. The number of farm laborers declined by a third, falling from 14 to 7 percent of all Spanish-surname workers in the Southwest. The labor and private household service categories accounted for 28 percent at the start of the decade, but only 17 percent at the end. The net shift was mainly to craft, clerical, and service jobs, with craftsmen going from 13 percent to 15 percent, clerks, secretaries and typists from 9 to 14 percent, and service workers from 10 to 14 percent.

These occupational shifts were somewhat greater in magnitude than for whites. Weighing the occupational distribution by average (1970) earnings in each occupation yields an average earnings index for Spanish-surname individuals. In the Southwest this index was 82 percent that for whites nationwide in 1960, rising to 86 percent in 1970. In contrast, persons with Spanish-surnames did not keep pace with black advances and the Chicano index declined from 111 to 105 percent of blacks. Also, the relative earnings index declined within the broad professional, managerial, and craft categories as Chicanos increasingly concentrated in the low earning occupations within each group.

Relative earnings improved noticeably, however, because of shifts to higher paying industries and firms, and perhaps because of reduced discrimination. Chicano laborers and operatives made the most significant gains (Table 13).

TABLE 13. RATIO OF SPANISH-SURNAME AND ANGLO MALE EARNINGS

	California		Texas	
	1959	1969	1959	1969
Professional	.84	.83	.60	.70
Managerial	.80	.90	.59	.64
Sales	.83	.93	.53	.65
Craft	.89	.90	.64	.68
Operatives	.88	.93	.58	.72
Laborers	1.03	2.20	.83	1.92

There were also improvements in employment status. For 25- to 34-year-old males the ratio of Spanish-surname to Anglo unemployment fell from 1.6 to 1.3; for females it declined from 1.6 to 1.4. The proportion of Spanish-surnamed family heads working 40 to 52 weeks rose from 71 to 74 percent. And between 1969 and 1973, despite the recession, there was no increase in the reported rate of unemployment among either Mexican-origin males or females.

Education

Mexican-Americans have serious educational deficiencies that are probably more severe than those of the other three minorities. Their 8.1 years median school attainment in

1970 lagged behind Indians and blacks by 1.7 years and Puerto Ricans by 0.6 years. Twenty- to 24-year olds are much better off with half completing high school, though this is still less than for blacks or Indians. Six of ten Mexican-American first graders can expect to graduate from high school compared with nine of ten Anglos, and more than three-fourths of Chicanos who make it to the twelfth grade are reading below the norm for their grade. Chicano students are twice as likely to be kept back to repeat a year and are seven times more likely than Anglos to be overage for their grade. Spanish-surname students nationwide represented two percent of full-time enrollment in colleges and universities in school year 1971, and 19 percent of total minority enrollment compared to their 30 percent population share among college aged minorities. In the Southwest they accounted for only one-fourteenth the enrollment in undergraduate institutions, less than half their proportionate share.

These problems testify to the severity of longstanding problems, not the lack of progress. In 1960 only 18 percent of Spanish-surname males aged 14 years and over in the Southwest had completed high school. A decade later the proportion had risen to 29 percent, with median attainment increasing 1.6 years. For females, attainment went up 1.4 years. Among 25- to 34-year olds of both sexes, only a fourth had completed high school in 1960, compared with nearly two-fifths in 1970. The result was a narrowing of racial differentials. In California the medan attainment of persons with Spanish-surname age 25 years and over went from 8.6 to 10.6 years, reducing the gap relative to Anglos from 3.6 to 1.8 years. In Texas, the Chicano attainment gain from 4.8 to 7.2 years reduced the gap from a staggering 6.6 to a still substantial 4.7 years. Less encouragingly, the proportion of the Spanish-surname population aged 14 years and over with a college degree increased only from 2 to 3 percent over the decade.

These educational gains apparently had a significant pay-off. In 1959 California Spanish-surname males with a high school education had an income 7 percent above that of dropouts; by 1969 the differential had increased to 13 percent. Those with college degrees received 24 percent more than those with only a high school diploma in 1959, but 36 percent more in 1969. For 1970-1973 Mexican-origin high school graduates aged 25 years and over nationwide had an average income 17 percent above dropouts and a fifth less than those with one or more years of college.

Family Status

In contrast to other minorities, the marital and family status of Mexican-Americans is not a cause for concern. Their families are stable and large. In 1970 Mexican-American ever-married women had given birth to an average of 4.5 children, or 1.0 more than Puerto Ricans, 0.7 more than than blacks, and 1.5 more than other whites. Yet fertility is declining both absolutely and relatively. Ever-married Chicano women age 25 to 34 years had 1.0 more children than the average U. S. women this age in 1960, but 0.7 more in 1970. The absolute reduction in fertility rates was greatest for the least educated, declining by a fourth among women with less than a high school education, slightly more for high school graduates, but only a fifth for college graduates (Chart 7).

Despite low income, urbanization, and limited education —the factors usually associated with the deterioration of the husband-wife unit — 86 percent of Mexican-origin families were headed by a male in 1973, only 2 percentage points

CHART 7. CHILDREN BORN PER 1,000 MARRIED WOMEN

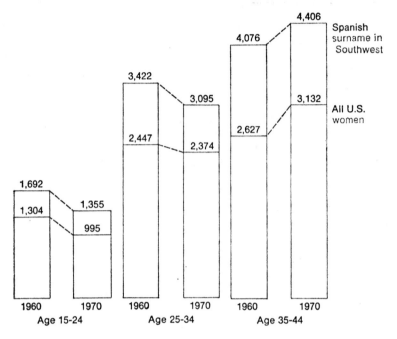

below the total population and 2 percentage points higher than among Chicanos in 1960.

Other Factors

Mexican-Americans also have distinct cultural and social traits which in some ways aid and in other ways hinder their socioeconomic advancement. With the constant influx of immigrants and culture from nearby Mexico, the Spanish language has not been quickly shed in the U. S. In 1970 Spanish was spoken in 70 percent of the Southwest homes whose head claimed Mexican origin; it was the principle language in more than half the homes. Language handicaps are more prevalent for the elderly, and young Chicanos are usually bilingual. Nonetheless, language barriers may continue to impede learning and labor market success at all age levels.

Other cultural traits are not easily quantified but are undoubtedly important. Studies generally conclude that Mexican-Americans stress individual and family relationships more than involvement in societal institutions, that there is greater male dominance in the family, and that the welfare of the family is given precedence over the welfare of the individual. To the extent these generalizations are valid, the Chicano culture may help rather than hinder integration into the mainstream: emphasis on family and work are coincident with the prevailing majority ethic and the apparent willingness to accept common labor and other menial jobs has not challenged the labor market status of the majority.

Whether for the above reasons or because Chicanos are usually white, they are less frequently the victims of discrimination than blacks. Chicano males earned 1.06 the median of blacks in California and 1.02 in Texas in 1969, but when adjusted for their substantially lesser education, Chicanos are clearly better off (Table 14).

TABLE 14. RATIO OF MEDIAN MALE INCOME SPANISH-SURNAME/BLACKS

Years of Schooling	California	Texas
9-11 years	1.32	1.30
12 years	1.23	1.26
16 years and over	1.21	1.18

Mexican-Americans are also far less segregated than blacks. In 35 southwestern cities the 1960 "index of discrimination," measuring the degree of segregation within census tracts (ranging from 0 in the case of perfect integration to 100 in the case of complete discrimination), was 55 when comparing Anglos and persons of Spanish surname, but 80 when comparing Anglos and blacks. (Interestingly, the index was 23 comparing Spanish-surname foreign born

with those native born). Almost all of the variation between
cities in the Mexican-American index of discrimination was
explained by the economic differences between Anglos and
Chicanos within these cities.

As another indicator, 44 percent of first grade Mexican-
American students attended school where they constituted
20 percent or less of the enrollment in 1966 compared with
10 percent of black students. At the 12th grade level, Mexican-American students were more likely than Indians, Puerto
Ricans, or blacks to be in schools where they represented
less than 20 percent of the population. In fact Chicanos have
had to press the federal government for recognition as a
separate and distinct racial group. In a suit won by a Chicano
interest group, a federal district court in Corpus Christi,
Texas, held in 1970 that Mexican-Americans were a separate
racial class and could not be counted as "white" in comply-
ing with integration requirements.

Perhaps because discrimination and segregation are less
extreme, or perhaps because of the cultural emphasis on
family rather than other social institutions, the political and
economic power of Mexican-Americans is limited. In the
1960s Chicanos displayed some political activism through
formation of La Raza Unida and Jobs for Progress-Opera-
tion SER (Services, Employment and Redevelopment). These
joined older groups such as the American GI Forum which
stressed the aims of middle-class Chicanos. Without gain-
saying the activities of such organizations, they had less
leverage and were less active than similar black groups.

The Republican party made an effort in the 1972 election
to attract traditionally Democratic Hispanics. A number of
highly visible appointments were made, as well as many
promises. Yet only 44 percent of the voting age Spanish-
origin population was registered in 1972 compared with 73
percent of all whites and 65 percent of blacks. The voting

rates among those registered were 84 percent for Hispanics compared with 88 percent for all whites. Obviously, the low voting record reduces the potential political clout.

Given their blue collar concentration, Mexican-Americans have gained some strength in unions. The efforts of the United Farm Workers and the recent Farah strike are only the most visible signs of union participation. In 1969 Spanish-surnamed constituted 7 percent of the total craft union membership with control over job assignments though they represented only 4 percent of all craftsmen. The Spanish-surname membership in building trade unions was due more to "market processes" than minority activism; Chicanos joined unions when they moved into blue collar unionized jobs and not because they forced their way in. Through 1973 all Hispanics accounted for 23 percent of the minority participants hired under Home Town plans, although they represent a much larger proportion of total minority blue collar workers. Apprenticeship programs have also focused more on blacks than Chicanos. And to date Mexican-American representation in the union leadership ranks has been even less than that of blacks.

Migration and Socioeconomic Gains

A decisive factor in improvements in income, education, and employment has been the geographic redistribution of the Mexican-American population. By both absolute and relative measures, Chicanos in California are better off than those in the border areas near Texas. At the time of the 1960 Census, Texas and California each accounted for two-fifths of the Southwest's Spanish-surname population. By 1970 California contained one-half and Texas one-third. Urbanization thoughout the area was also significant. In 1950 and 1960, Anglos were more urbanized than Chicanos; by 1970 this had reversed as a result of a 60 percent decline in the Chicano rural farm population and a 45 percent increase in urban residents. By 1970, 84 percent of persons with Mexican birth or parentage lived in metropolitan areas and 47 percent resided in central cities compared with 69 and 31 percent, respectively, among all persons in the Southwest.

For most population groups, the urbanization process is associated with rising income, more stable employment (especially for females), increased school enrollment and attainment, reductions in fertility, and increases in female headed families. To varying degrees, these patterns have held true for Mexican-Americans.

The mean income of urban males of Mexican origin in 1969 was a third higher than for rural nonfarm males and three-fifths higher than for those in farm areas. Among females, the urban mean was two-fifths above the rural nonfarm and 52 percent more than the rural farm mean.

Greater labor market opportunities were a prime factor. The labor force participation rate of females was 38 percent in all urban areas, but 28 percent in rural areas. Where 32 percent of males were employed as professionals, managers, and craftsmen in urban areas, only 21 percent of males in nonfarm rural areas found such jobs; 35 percent of urban women worked as professionals, managers, or clerks compared with 25 percent in rural nonfarm areas.

Urban Chicanos have completed much more school. The medians among 25- to 34-year-old males were 11.0 years for urbanites, 8.7 years for those in rural nonfarm areas, and 7.5 for those in rural farm areas in 1970. The proportions with a high school diploma were 38, 29, and 23 percent, respectively.

Fertility patterns also differ. Among Mexican-origin ever-married women aged 25 to 34, the average number of chil-

dren was 3.6 in rural nonfarm areas and 3.9 in rural farm
areas, compared with 3.1 in urban areas.

The negative aspects of urbanization — greater instability
and dependency — are evident also. One in seven urban
families (one in six in the five cities with the largest number
of Chicanos) was headed by a female compared with one in
ten in rural nonfarm areas and one in twenty in rural farm
areas. The proportion of Mexican-origin children living with
both parents was 79 percent in urban areas but 84 percent
in rural nonfarm and 88 percent in rural farm areas. While
only 12 percent of urban Chicano families received public
assistance — the same as in rural nonfarm areas and only
slightly above the 9 percent in rural farm areas — recipients represented 47 percent of the poor in the first case but
only 29 and 23 percent, respectively, in the latter two.

The Absorption Process

Though Mexican-Americans were here before the first
Anglo settlers, immigrants account for a large share of the
current population, and a substantial portion of its recent
growth. In the 1950s, 300,000 legal immigrants joined the
750,000 who had come earlier; an additional 443,000 im-
migrated in the next decade. By 1970 one in six persons of
Spanish-surname in the Southwest was foreign born. Only
two-fifths of these immigrants were U. S. citizens. Second
generation immigrants — U. S. born with foreign or mixed
parentage — accounted for an additional three in ten persons of Spanish surname.

	1960	1970
Spanish-surname in Southwest	3,465	4,544
U.S. born parentage	1,899	2,514
Foreign or mixed parentage	1,031	1.303
Foreign born	535	727

There are significant differences between the first, second, and third (or later) generation Mexican-Americans. U. S. born Spanish-American women have lower birth rates than immigrants. Third generation ever-married women aged 25 to 34 years had had an average of 3.1 children in 1970, compared with 3.3 for other Mexican-American women this age. Immigrant Chicano women aged 35 to 44 had had 4.8 children, compared to 4.7 for second generation and 4.4 for third generation. On the other hand, third generation families were slightly more likely to be headed by females:

PERCENTAGE OF FAMILIES WITH FEMALE HEAD

	20-24	25-34	35-44
Born in Mexico	10.2	9.6	12.5
U.S. born of Mexican parentage	10.6	10.4	12.6
U.S. born of U.S. born parentage	12.1	12.4	14.0

Second generation Mexican-Americans are substantiallly better educated than those born in Mexico, but the gap between second and third (or later) generations is much less, with the median years of schooling for 20- to 24-year olds almost identical (Chart 8).

Labor force participation patterns differ between generations, with male natives of native parentage slightly less likely, but females more likely, to work than the Mexican born. More than two-fifths of 25- to 34-year-old second and third generation women were in the labor force in 1970 compared with a third of immigrants.

A substantial occupational upgrading occurs between the first and second generations, but there is less advancement thereafter. Among employed 25- to 34-year-olds, 35 percent of the Mexican born are laborers, farm, or service workers compared with 24 percent for second generation and 25 percent for third generation. The same pattern prevails for 35- to 44-year-olds, with 41 percent of the Mexican

CHART 8. MEDIAN YEARS OF SCHOOL COMPLETED, 1970

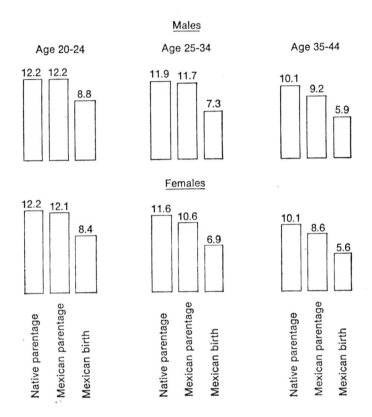

Males

Age 20-24   Age 25-34   Age 35-44

12.2 12.2   11.9 11.7   10.1
         8.8   11.7   9.2
                            7.3   5.9

Females

12.2 12.1   11.6   10.1
         8.4   10.6   8.6
                            6.9   5.6

Native parentage   Mexican parentage   Mexican birth

born, but 27 percent of the second and third generation workers in these low level categories.

Among males, there are substantial differences between the median earnings of the foreign and native born, but much smaller differences between second and third generation. For women, however, there is a progression between the three generations.

Quite obviously, then, the assimilation process is occurring. The sons and daughters of immigrants are substantially better off than their mothers and fathers. Birth rates are reduced significantly as more second and third genera-

MEDIAN EARNINGS AS A PROPORTION OF MEDIAN FOR THIRD GENERATION

	Age 20-24	Age 25-34	Age 35-44
Male			
Second generation	96%	100%	99%
Mexican born	88	82	82
Female			
Second generation	95	95	94
Mexican born	92	90	86

tion women enter the labor force and become breadwinners with only a slight strain on marital stability.

On a less positive note, the second to third generation changes in education, occupation, and earnings for males are not of a very great magnitude. The available evidence suggests that an increase in the proportion of Mexican-Americans whose parents were born in the U. S. will not, alone, be a major factor in improving the overall status of Chicano men.

Border Issues

Since the Mexican-American population is concentrated close to the Mexican border, the status of U. S. citizens is vitally affected by the flow of legal and illegal immigrants as well as the competition for jobs from Mexican residents and Mexican firms. Nowhere in the world are there such drastic economic differences between neighboring nations as at the U. S. - Mexican border. To the degree that the door is open for immigration from Mexico, there will be an abundant supply of workers competing for jobs with U. S. citizens and residents. National border policies are, therefore, of vital importance to Mexican-Americans.

From 1942 through 1964 Mexican citizens were imported temporarily on a contract basis to work in agriculture. These "braceros," numbering over 400,000 annually in the late 1950s, depressed the wages of native agricultural workers. The termination of the program in 1964 had some positive impact. Yet the number of braceros had already declined to 200,000 by 1962, since mechanization was reducing the demand and since there was an excess U. S.-based labor supply which could be hired without paying for transportation, food, and lodging. In any case, subsequent minimum wage coverage of agriculture would have undermined the value of imported low-wage workers.

The United States imposed a ceiling on Mexican immigration in 1968 when an annual limit of 120,000 was imposed on all Western Hemisphere nations. Despite this limit Mexican migration continued to rise reaching 50,000 immigrants in 1971 compared to the 40,000 annual average for fiscal 1965 through 1968. Of the 15,300 family heads, four of every five planned to reside in either California or Texas, an equal proportion were laborers or service workers, and less than 4 percent were professional and technical workers. While the new immigrants added annually only about one percent to the Mexican-origin work force in these states, they accounted for a larger share of the growth in the number of unskilled.

In addition to the permanent and other temporary migration, another form of bracero program continues. In 1972 an estimated 735,000 legal entrees in this country were "green carders" who had been admitted, at least in theory, to fill labor shortages. Their residence in the U. S. depended on continued employment. "Green carders," unlike permanent resident immigrants, may move back to Mexico and reenter the United States at will. In 1969 an estimated 50,000 crossed the border daily, enjoying the lower living costs in Mexico and, in many cases, failing to pay U. S. income taxes. Their competition depressed the wage levels in communities within daily commuting distance of the border.

Not only do Mexican residents compete for U. S. jobs, but Mexican sites compete for U. S. firms. The 1965 Border

Industrial Program limited tariffs to the value added in the assembly of products manufactured in the U. S. for plants located within 12½ miles of the border. With wages in Mexico's border towns averaging $4.00 daily compared with the then $12.80 U. S. minimum wage, a number of firms found it profitable to locate in Mexico. By 1972 there were 345 plants employing 46,000 workers participating in the program. If these plants were located on the U. S. side of the border, Mexican-Americans would be more likely to benefit (though it is not certain that the firms would have located in the Southwest in the absence of the program or that U. S. citizens would have necessarily been hired).

The critical issue, however, is not the regulated sources of labor competition, but rather the flood of illegal immigration. Mexicans may cross the border unchecked in a number of places. Alternatively, "white cards" can be acquired to travel up to 72 hours within a 25-mile radius of the border for business or pleasure, though not for employment. However, the employment restrictions are difficult to enforce given the free mobility within the United States. Once in the country the Mexican "tourist" can get lost in the crowd in the large cities of the Southwest. A common practice is to get a job and mail the white card back to Mexico. If caught and returned to Mexico, the card will be waiting for a return trip. In less than 5 percent of the cases where an illegal is discovered are formal proceedings undertaken which would make reentry a felony.

Illegal immigration is economically motivated. It is made possible by the availability of jobs for illegals. Although the importation of illegal aliens has been a felony since 1952, the law is not enforced and an employer who hires illegal immigrants does so apparently with impunity unless he violates social security, minimum wage, or tax laws.

Identification is a major problem since social security cards have generally been available to all applicants without any check on citizenship status. The Social Security Act of 1972 required that steps be taken to insure that only citizens or legal workers get cards, but it remains to be seen how stringently this will be enforced. Social Security cards, like immigration papers, may also be falsified.

There is no way to determine the magnitude of illegal immigration or the number of illegals in the country at any point in time. From 1965 through 1972 an average of 200,-000 illegals were returned to Mexico each year, with the number reaching 400,000 in 1972. One informed estimate is that for every illegal returned, another enters the country. If there are, indeed, more than 400,000 illegals in the Southwest, and if most are workers, this has a massive impact, since there were only 683,000 employed persons of Spanish origin in the area in 1970.

Prospects

• The rate of immigration will be crucial to the well-being of Mexican-Americans who are already in the United States. While illegal immigration cannot be stopped, it can certainly be slowed. Increases and extension of the minimum wage may push up the floor for employers so that it is less profitable to hire the unskilled, reducing the attractiveness of foreign workers. More vigorous certification for social security cards may be useful and proof of citizenship might be required for all employment. Though work papers would be a burden to Mexican-Americans, they would also help to improve their labor market status. Substantial financial and criminal penalties on employers accompanied by more rigorous enforcement would also reduce the incentives to hire illegals.

- Mexican-Americans will be disproportionately affected by changing employment prospects in the Southwest and in the blue collar occupations generally. Urbanization has had its major payoffs and is not likely to be a significant factor in the future. Regional redistribution, however, may occur.

- Mexican-Americans, with their work orientation and relatively stable family structure can, in all likelihood, be absorbed into the economic mainstream once they acquire the needed skills and credentials. There is likely to be a continued high payoff on education. But if Mexican-Americans are to break into the upper income quintile in large numbers, increased college attendance is vital.

- The future progress of Mexican-Americans depends on whether their cultural strengths will endure the pressures of low income, improved female labor market status, more readily available welfare, and other influences which have dramatically affected urbanized Puerto Ricans and blacks. Birth rates are likely to decline, but dependency and female-headed families may rise.

Mexican-Americans have gained in the last decade by capitalizing on their cultural strengths and taking advantage of available opportunities. They have improved their position by moving to urban areas, upgrading into better paying operative and crafts jobs, as well as by expanding the number of working wives. Though progress was not as rapid in all aspects as that for some other minority groups, the greater payoffs for education, and the improved status of second and third generation individuals, promise that gains will continue at a steady, if slower, pace in the future. Over a longer period the complete economic assimilation and equality of Mexican-American appears possible.

IV

PUERTO RICANS

Despite common language and Hispanic origin, the shared
experience of immigration, and many similar socioeconomic
problems, Puerto Ricans differ in several important ways
from Chicanos: first, they are more recent immigrants and
are still in the early stages of adjustment; second, they have
distinct cultural characteristics manifest in their differing
marital and family patterns; third, they are even more urbanized and concentrated in the largest northeastern cities;
and fourth, while Mexican-Americans are a step above blacks
and Indians in the Southwest, Puerto Ricans are the bottom
stratum in the areas where they are concentrated.

Geography, Demography, and Status

The census counted 1.4 million persons of Puerto Rican
birth or parentage in 1970, consisting mostly of first or
second generation immigrants who have come to the mainland since the end of World War II. The Puerto Rican population tripled in the 1950s and increased 56 percent in the
1960s, with two-thirds of the population growth in the first
decade, and two-fifths in the second, resulting from net immigration. In 1970 three-fifths of all Puerto Ricans and six-
sevenths of those over 21 were immigrants. Almost three-
fourths reported speaking Spanish currently in the home.
Puerto Ricans are highly concentrated. Three-fifths lived
in New York City in 1970, the vast majority in the Bronx
and east Harlem. There had been, however, some dispersion

CHART 9. THE PUERTO RICAN POPULATION (THOUSANDS)

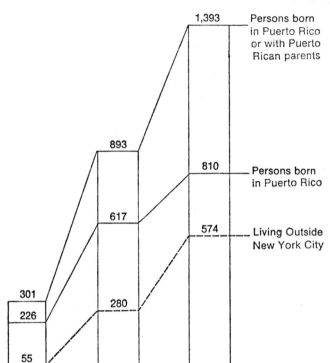

during the 1960s, with the proportion living in New York declining from 69 to 59 percent. To a large extent, this occurred because many new and recent immigrants moved to areas outside New York. Over the decade, the city accounted for two-fifths of the Puerto Rican population growth but less than a fourth of the increase in persons of Puerto Rican birth (Chart 9).

This latest wave of newcomers to the U. S. lags substantially behind national averages in almost all dimensions of socioeconomic status, and even farther behind those in the New York Standard Metropolitan Statistical Area (SMSA).

The litany of woes is by now familiar. Birth rates are high, with Puerto Rican women aged 35 to 44 averaging 3.2 children or a third more than all New Yorkers. Education is deficient, with less than a fourth of those aged 25 years and over having a high school diploma compared with nearly three-fifths in standard metropolitan area. Unemployment rates are half again national averages, and the nonworker/worker ratio in families is nearly double the city average. Family income is 56 percent of the metropolitan and 64 percent of the national median. A third of Puerto Rican children and youths below age 18 are growing up in broken homes, double the national average.

The gravity of these problems is perhaps better illustrated by comparing Puerto Ricans with blacks and other neighbors in the low-income areas where they reside. The 1970 Census Employment Survey collected data for seven poverty areas in New York City; one in four residents were Puerto Rican (accounting for almost half of all Puerto Ricans in the United States). By most measures, their problems were even more severe than those of their neighbors. The unemployment rate for Puerto Rican males was 1.3 times that of all poverty area males, and only 7 percent of those employed were in professional, technical, and managerial jobs, two-fifths the percentage among all residents. The weekly median salary of full-time working Puerto Rican males was 88 percent of the poverty area average, and a third of the Puerto Rican families with male heads were poor. Nearly a fourth of husband-wife families and 82 percent of those headed by females were on welfare, compared with 13 and 65 percent, respectively, of all poverty area families. Three in ten Puerto Ricans aged 25 to 34 had completed less than 8 grades of education.

Clearly, Puerto Ricans are among the most disadvantaged even in the poverty neighborhoods where they are concentrated. Since they are much more likely to live in high-wage but high-cost areas, where welfare may exceed average wages for the unskilled in other parts of the country, their relative status appears better in national comparisons than it really is.

Developments Since 1960

The experience of Puerto Ricans since 1960 is similar to that of other minorities. Improved educational attainment has led to occupational upgrading and higher earnings, but the gaps between Puerto Ricans and whites have narrowed only modestly. Relative income improved during the 1960s but stagnated subsequently. A notable negative development was the deterioration of the family.

Median years of school completed by 20- to 24-year-old Puerto Ricans rose 1.8 years over the 1960s; for 25- to 34-year olds it rose 1.4, and for 35- to 44-year olds, 0.8. The proportion of 20- 24-year olds with one or more years of college doubled from one in twenty to one in ten. The relative gains are reflected in the narrowing "diploma gap." In 1960, whites age 25 to 34 were three times more likely to be high school graduates than Puerto Ricans, but only twice as likely in 1974:

PERCENT 25-TO-35-YEAR OLDS COMPLETED HIGH SCHOOL

	Whites	Puerto Ricans
1960	61	21
1970	76	30
1974	82	40

Labor market trends have been mixed. The proportion of males employed in professional, managerial, and craft jobs increased over the 1960s from 17 to 26 percent among 25- to 34-year olds and from 21 to 27 percent among 35- to 44-year olds. Females recorded greater progress. The proportion of Puerto Rican females employed in professional, managerial, and clerical jobs rose from 19 to 38 percent among the younger cohort and from 14 to 29 percent for the older group. Despite these occupational advances, employment status did not improve. In line with the experience of other minority groups, labor force participation of males declined not only among youths and workers past prime working age, but also among 25- to 34-year-old men for whom the rates fell from 92 to 87 percent, closely paralleling the drop for blacks. In contrast to national and other minority trends, however, participation of Puerto Rican women also declined, with the rate for 25- to 34-year olds falling from 39 to 29 percent. While unemployment rates for all age/sex cohorts dropped in the 1960s, the overall rate for Puerto Rican males rose from 5.6 to 11.1 percent between 1970 and 1973. Meanwhile, the proportion employed the rapidly growing professional, technical, managerial, and craft jobs fell slightly, while that in laborer and service occupations increased by several percentage points.

The median income of Puerto Rican families in the New York metropolitan area rose from 58 to 60 percent of the metropolitan median between 1959 and 1969, but because New York grew more slowly than the rest of the nation, the New York Puerto Rican median fell from 67 to 59 percent of the national median. While the income of males tended to rise relative to U. S. whites of the same age and sex, the relative position of Puerto Rican females declined:

PUERTO RICAN MEDIAN INCOME AS PERCENT OF U.S. MEDIAN

	1959	1969
25-34-year-old		
Males	66	71
Females	119	109
35-44-year-old		
Males	63	66
Females	120	107

Declining relative earnings and decreased labor force participation of women, coupled with growing numbers of female-headed families curtailed the growth of Puerto Rican family income. In contrast to black families whose income gains depended greatly on female earnings contributions, Puerto Rican advances depended mostly on increased male earnings and welfare payments. A significant proportion of average Puerto Rican family income resulted from the comparatively high New York welfare payments, which partly accounts for the relatively high median income of Puerto Rican women.

Puerto Rican median family income rose from $6,165 in 1969 to $6,779 in 1973, but this matched neither the cost-of-living increase nor the rise in the income of other groups. The $600 rise marked a 9 percent drop in constant dollars and their median income declined from 62 to 56 percent of the U. S. median. Their incidence of poverty rose from 30 to 34 percent.

Marital and family status changes were a cause for concern. Among women age 25 to 34 years in 1960, one in ten were family heads; a decade later, the proportion was one in four. The trend toward family deterioration apparently accelerated during the 1970s. By March 1974 one of every three Puerto Rican families was headed by a woman.

First and Second Generation Changes

Other immigrant groups started off at the bottom of the socioeconomic system relegated to the nation's slums and its dirty work until they were assimilated into the mainstream. Since it is clear that Puerto Ricans have started at the bottom, the critical issue is whether they are following the same upward path.

Second generation Puerto Ricans are substantially better

off than immigrants in terms of income, employment, and education (Table 15). Mainland-born males aged 25 to 34 years had completed 12.1 years of school in 1970 and had a median income of $6,835; immigrant males this age averaged two years less school and a median income almost a fifth lower. Differentials were wider among 35- to 44-year olds and narrower among 20- to 24-year olds. Immigrant Puerto Ricans are also more frequently the victims of unemployment.

TABLE 15. EDUCATION, INCOME, AND UNEMPLOYMENT
AMONG IMMIGRANTS AND U. S. BORN PUERTO RICANS, 1970

	Age 25-34		Age 35-44	
	Immi-grants	*U.S. born*	*Immi-grants*	*U.S. born*
Median years school completed	9.6	12.1	8.4	11.6
Median Income				
Males	$5,577	$6,835	$5,803	$7,700
Females	3,216	3,748	3,422	3,976
Unemployment rate (percent)				
Males	5.6	4.9	4.6	4.2
Females	9.1	5.1	6.7	3.6

Marital and family patterns also differ (Table 16). Puerto Rican women born in the continental U. S. have fewer children. They are less likely to be married, or to become divorced or separated once married. As a result, 19 percent of families with mainland-born parents received public assistance in 1970, compared to 25 percent of families headed by an immigrant. One indicator of assimilation is the degree of racial intermarriage. Roughly half of mainland born women have a non-Puerto Rican spouse compared with only a sixth of those born on the island.

Puerto Ricans outside New York City tend to be better off than those who remain, having higher income, more stable families, and greater educational attainment. So far, however, the mobility of Puerto Rican families living within the continental United States has not been a major factor in their overall gains. Seventy percent of the U. S.-born Puerto Ricans outside of New York in 1970 lived in their state of birth, i.e. they had not migrated within the U. S. Half of Island-born Puerto Ricans outside New York who had moved in the last five years came directly from Puerto Rico. This suggests that population growth outside New York is due less to internal migration than to changing immigration patterns, though relocation is undoubtedly a route upward for some.

TABLE 16. MARITAL AND FAMILY PATTERNS
OF IMMIGRANTS AND U.S. BORN PUERTO RICANS, 1970

	Age 20-24		Age 25-34		Age 35-44	
	Immi-grants	*U.S. born*	*Immi-grants*	*U.S. born*	*Immi-grants*	*U.S. born*
Percent families headed by women	27.0	22.1	25.0	23.0	23.3	19.3
Children born per 1,000 ever-married women	1,507	1,074	2,812	2,272	3,563	3,007
Percent of females married with non-Puerto Rican spouse	14.7	38.8	15.3	49.4	15.7	50.3

Is the "Melting Pot" Cooking?

These trends suggest that Puerto Ricans as a group are advancing slowly toward national income and employment norms. Though educational gains have been notable, the deterioration of the family has been a countervailing force. More optimistically, comparisons of mainland- and Island-born Puerto Ricans suggest that assimilation is occurring with the second generation finding better jobs, earning more money, going farther in school, and having fewer children and more stable families. These contrasting views are not contradictory. Over the 1960s the proportion of Puerto Ricans who were born in the continental U. S. rose from 31 to 42 percent, but the rise among the older cohorts was even less. The changing proportions of mainland- and Island-born were not great enough to noticeably change average socio-economic status. As the younger native born generation ages, the averages might be expected to rise more rapidly.

In some dimensions, however, this optimism is not warranted. Although female-headed families are less prevalent in the second generation, their number increased dramatically during the last 15 years among both mainland-born and immigrant families. The key factors determining the future advancement will be payoff on education, the third generation experience, and the extent to which legal and illegal immigrants from Latin American countries provide competition to Puerto Ricans in the labor market.

• There is no way to know whether the benefits of increased schooling will continue in the future. All evidence indicates, however, that education still has a payoff as high school graduates earn more than workers with less education:

Years of School	Median Income
12 years or more	100%
9-11 years	78
8 years	70
5-7 years	68
0-4 years	54

• Observations on future trends must be speculative since there are few third-generation Puerto Ricans in the continental U. S. Only 1.43 million persons identified themselves as of Puerto Rican origin in 1970, compared to 1.39 million who reported Puerto Rican birth or parentage, suggesting that there were few third-generation Puerto Ricans. The high

rate of intermarriage suggests that the experience of the off-
spring may be significantly different than that of the mainland-born parents. Since Puerto Ricans are at the bottom
of the socioeconomic stratum, they are undoubtedly "marry-
ing-up" on the average.

• The most disadvantaged Puerto Ricans tend to return
to the Island, especially after they become eligible for unemployment compensation or social security. An increased or
decreased rate of outflow could affect averages for those remaining. On the other hand, if large numbers of Puerto
Ricans come into the country because of depressed conditions
on the island, this might reduce the opportunities for those
already here, certainly lowering the average indicators of
socioconomic status. Immigration has been much slower of
late. However, a current uncertainty is the influx of illegals
from other Caribbean nations who work in sweat shop conditions at low wages and depress the wage structure. The
increases in labor supply willing to accept low wages adversely affects the job prospects of Puerto Ricans and their
potential gains in the labor market.

In summary, then, the melting pot seems to be working in
the traditional ways of gradually improving education, occupational status, and earnings, and reducing birth rates. There
are a number of less desirable spillovers, such as the accelerated deterioration of the family and rising dependency,
which may undermine future advancement. Yet the evidence
justifies a degree of optimism. The "melting" process, while
slow, is underway.

V

INDIANS

Although American Indians appear to share the same hardships as other minorities — poverty, unemployment, deficient education, discrimination — Indians are unique in many ways, most crucially in their isolation on reservations and their dependency on the federal government. For example, the causes and cures of widespread unemployment among reservation Indians are far more complex than those of Indians or other minorities in urban areas. On reservations it is not a question of discrimination or lack of education foreclosing opportunities — the jobs simply do not exist. Similarly, the problem of bringing quality education to Indians is less one of ending segregation or equalizing resource allocations than of building, staffing, and supplying schools to serve the isolated and culturally diverse Indian population.

In these and other problems the pre-eminent role of the federal government is a matter for scrutiny. The Bureau of Indian Affairs and other federal agencies have responsibility for Indian education, health, housing, social services, land management, public works, and a multitude of other services. Moreover, these agencies directly provide over two-fifths of all jobs and three-fifths of all income on reservations. The success or failure of federal programs greatly determines the quality of Indian lives.

Indian Demography*

In 1970, 827,000 people identified themselves as Indians,

Eskimos, or Aleuts. In 1973 the Bureau of Indian Affairs (BIA), which has responsibility only for those living on or near reservations, estimated than 543,000 Indians, Eskimos, and Aleuts in the 25 reservation states were eligible for its services, suggesting that a majority still live close to their reservations. More than three of every four Indians were located west of the Mississippi: the largest numbers reside in Arizona, New Mexico, Oklahoma, California, and Alaska. Though there are 481 identified tribal entities in the United States, a majority belong to just ten tribes of whom the Navajo, Cherokee, Sioux, and Chippewa tribes were by far the largest.

The customs, social and economic conditions, as well as the legal status of these tribes vary so widely that generalizations are hazardous. The largest tribe, the Navajos, reside mostly on or near their reservation, maintaining their traditions and generally participating little in white society. By contrast, few of the second largest tribe, the Cherokees, live on their reservation in North Carolina. With education and family income nearly twice as high as those of Navajos, the Cherokees clearly are far more assimilated into the social and economic mainstream.

Since World War II the lure of employment opportunities and federal policy encouraging migration have drawn increasing numbers of Indians from reservations to the cities. Between 1960 and 1970 the census count of urban Indians more than doubled from 165,000 to 340,000, compared to

---

*The two major sources of data on Indians, the Bureau of Indian Affairs and the Bureau of the Census, use different definitions and methods of collecting their statistics. The census counts all Indians who identify themselves as such. The Bureau of Indian Affairs counts only those who live on or near reservations. This difference makes cross-checking, interchanging, or comparing the two sets of data impossible. Since each source provides information unavailable elsewhere it is necessary to use both, whatever apparent inconsistency this may entail.

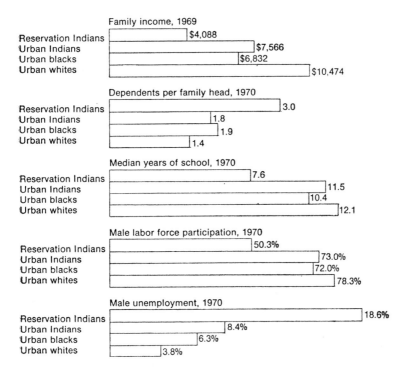

CHART 10. ECONOMIC AND SOCIAL INDICATORS FOR
RESERVATION INDIANS, URBAN INDIANS, BLACKS AND WHITES*

Family income, 1969
Reservation Indians $4,088
Urban Indians $7,566
Urban blacks $6,832
Urban whites $10,474

Dependents per family head, 1970
Reservation Indians   3.0
Urban Indians   1.8
Urban blacks   1.9
Urban whites   1.4

Median years of school, 1970
Reservation Indians   7.6
Urban Indians   11.5
Urban blacks   10.4
Urban whites   12.1

Male labor force participation, 1970
Reservation Indians   50.3%
Urban Indians   73.0%
Urban blacks   72.0%
Urban whites   78.3%

Male unemployment, 1970
Reservation Indians   18.6%
Urban Indians   8.4%
Urban blacks   6.3%
Urban whites   3.8%

*Residing in standard metropolitan statistical areas

the 11 percent growth in rural areas from 380,000 to 423,-
000. By 1970 Los Angeles, Tulsa, and Oklahoma City, among
others, had larger Indian populations than any reservation
except the Navajo.

Indians off the reservation present a startling contrast with
those who remain behind (Chart 10). Urban Indians are far
better educated, have much lower unemployment rates, two-
thirds greater average family income, fewer dependent children, and half the chance of being in poverty as those on
reservations. In fact, by such standards as family income,
male labor force participation, percent of high school grad-

uates, dependents per bread winner, and poverty status, Indians in metropolitan areas are better off than metropolitan blacks.

In contrast, Indians on reservations suffer the worst economic conditions of any group in the United States. Per capita income for rural Indians in 1969 was $1,147, two-fifths that of rural whites and a third that of all whites. Among Indians residing within reservation boundaries, median family income was only $4,088. With large families, per capita income on reservations was even lower — averaging only $962 in 1969, the lowest of any minority and less than a third of the average of whites. Fifty-five percent of all reservation Indians were living in poverty. However, limited data available indicate that poverty on Indian reservations may have been slightly alleviated since 1960. For example, between 1959 to 1969 the relative income of rural Indian males compared to rural whites rose from .31 to .50.

Poverty has many dimensions, but one of the most visible signs of deprivation is housing. Indian reservations have been aptly characterized as "open air slums." In 1973 the BIA housing survey found that out of 107,000 Indian families, 66,000 needed housing assistance. According to the 1970 census, 44 percent of all rural Indian households lived in housing with more than one person per room. Half had no bathroom, and a third lacked any interior water supply. One-third of all rural Indian households lived in homes over 30 years old, and two-thirds of all dwellings were valued at less than $7,500. In this regard, Indians are worse off than any other population group.

The economic picture would be even worse if it were not for government job creation. Forty-six percent of all jobs on Indian reservations are state, local, and federal positions, delivering the services provided by the BIA, the Indian Health Service, and other agencies. This percentage is more than three times the national average for government employment. By contrast, employment rates in wholesale and retail trade and in manufactuing are far below proportions common in the rest of the economy. Though Indian lands comprise the chief natural resource on reservations, farming and forestry employ only one-tenth of Indian men, and this proportion is declining.

Education

Measured by years of school completed and standardized for area of residence, Indians are better educated than other American minorities, but still less schooled than whites:

MEDIAN EDUCATION PERSONS AGE 25 AND OLDER, 1970

	Indian	Black	Mexican-American	White
Total	9.8	9.8	8.1	12.1
Urban	11.2	10.2	8.3	12.2
Rural nonfarm	8.7	7.7	6.2	11.6
Rural farm	8.4	7.2	5.4	11.0

Thirty-three percent of Indians over age 25 have graduated from high school, compared to 55 percent of whites and 31 percent of blacks. Since 1950 the proportion of Indian males with less than five years of school has fallen from one-third to one-eighth, while the proportion who are high school graduates has increased by exactly the reverse proportions. But, while Indian males have added an average of 2.7 years to their schooling, white males have added 3.1 years, so that gaps have not narrowed overall. Young Indians recorded some progress. Enrollment rates of Indians age 5 through 17 have been brought close to national averages, but completion rates have not improved commensurately. In 1970, 57 percent of Indian males aged 20 to 24 years had graduated from high school, a smaller proportion that the

63 percent of blacks and far below the 85 percent rate for whites. On reservations the dropout rate was even more severe, with less than half of rural Indian men aged 20 to 24 years having finished high school. Further, Indian high school seniors in 1966 lagged more than three grades in achievement relative to white norms.

More optimistically, increasing numbers are going on to college. Over 14,000 Indians were enrolled in college in March 1970 compared with only 2,000 Indian college graduates. Still, only 12 percent of Indians aged 18 to 24 years were in college in 1970, compared to 15 percent of blacks and 27 percent of whites.

The Population Explosion

The plight of Indians is made more critical because population growth on reservations far surpasses the economic gains. The Indian population is growing at 3 percent per year, faster than any population subgroup in the United States. Indian birth and fertility rates were nearly double those for whites in 1970 and were a third higher than those for nonwhites.

	Indians	Whites	Non-Whites
Birth Rate (per 1,000 population)	32.8	17.3	25.3
Fertility Rate (per 1,000 women aged 15-44 years)	155.0	83.9	114.3

While both white and nonwhite birth rates have dropped steadily since the 1950s, the Indian rate has leveled off after dipping slightly from its peak in the early 1960s. The large numbers of Indian women reaching child bearing age plus continued improvements in health care which will lengthen Indian life spans may be expected to boost population growth over the next decade.

INDIANS 87

The consequences are continued poverty and deprivation. For each potential Indian male breadwinner between age 25 and 54 years, there are 4.1 potential dependents under 19 years, while for the population as a whole, there are only 2.2. Already economically disadvantaged, reservation Indians have, on the average, twice as many mouths to feed as whites. Indian families tended to be larger than either those of whites or blacks. Nineteen percent of all Indian families have more than seven persons, compared to 15 percent of black and 5 percent of whites.

Obstacles to Progress

Indian culture and social relationships are distinct in many ways. Without minimizing the positive aspects, there are certain negative dimensions of vital importance which cannot be ignored in assessing socioeconomic status.

The Indian family, while not deteriorating as fast as that of blacks or Puerto Ricans, is less stable than that of whites. In 1970, 18 percent of all Indian familes were headed by women, a figure double the rate for whites but two-thirds of that for blacks (Table 17). Apparently, however, the changes of the 1960s did not seriously affect Indian family structure. The proportion of women over twenty with husbands present was stable, and female-headed families increased by only 2 percent.

TABLE 17. FAMILY STRUCTURE, 1970

	Indian	Black	White
Female-headed families	18 %	27 %	9 %
Children living with both parents	69	67	91
Women, age 20 and over			
Single	13	15	10
Husband absent, separated, divorced, widowed	27	38	21
Average number of persons per family	4.5	4.1	3.5

Despite the expansion of free health care on reservations by the Indian Health Service, severe health problems persist. Adjusted for age, Indian death rates from accidents and most diseases are higher than for the population as a whole. The differentials range from the five times greater likelihood of death from cirrhosis of the liver to the double risk of mortality from diabetes. A particular problem is accidental death (most often in motor vehicles), which is three times more common among Indians and is the second leading cause of Indian mortality. Although the published raw data do not show the interrelationship, the most important common thread which seems to unite the rising rates and higher likelihoods of certain causes of death is alcohol. Accidents, suicides, homicides, and, of course, cirrhosis of the liver have been reported by the Indian Health Service to be commonly alcohol-related. Each of these problems has been on the rise since federal laws prohibiting the sale of liquor to reservation Indians were repealed in 1953. At the same time, social problems reported to be related to alcohol, such as abandonment and crime, have also increased. There can be no doubt that alcoholism is a major problem on reservations.

For many types of crimes, law enforcement problems on Indian reservations are greater than those in other rural areas. Overall, reservation rates for the seven most serious crimes were about 63 percent greater than for the rural population as a whole. Crimes of violence are far more common among Indians, possibly a concommitant of drinking problems, while property crimes are less than half as likely among Indians as among other rural Americans.

Indians and the Federal Government

Individually, Indians were accorded full citizenship rights

in 1924. At present, the only major difference in Indian status regards the tribal or individual lands held in trust by the federal government. Neither these lands nor the income derived from them are subject to state and local taxation, and they may not be sold or transferred without the approval of federal officials. Indian tribes have the right to establish conditions for tribal membership, to choose their form of government, to levy taxes, to regulate domestic relations, to set property laws, and to administer justice for lesser crimes.

Within these broad parameters, federal policy toward Indians has zigzagged between the conflicting aims of assimilation and separation. Initially, Indians were to be segregated in designated areas and provided for as wards of the government. Almost as soon as the process of placing the Indians on reservations had been completed, policy shifted to encouraging their assimilation into society at large. Indians on reservations were encouraged to abandon tribal traditions, and an educational system aiming to instill white culture was developed. In 1887 Congress adopted a policy of alloting plots of up to 160 acres of Indian lands to "competent" Indian individuals. It was hoped that these Indian farmers would develop the self-sufficiency to grow out of their dependent federal status. This allotment policy continued for nearly 50 years despite the fact that it did not have the desired effect. As a result, three-fifths of all Indian land was lost as many Indians receiving allotments sold out to whites. Indian policies were revamped in 1934 when steps were begun to end allotment and to encourage the development of the Indian educational system and the reestablishment of Indian self-government. After World War II, however, sentiment again developed for terminating the federal government's special relationship with Indians, culminating in 1953 with the passage of a congressional resolution which declared termination to be the official federal policy. During the next five years, the trust status of a number of tribes was ended, including the Menominees in Wisconsin, the Klamaths in Oregon, and several tribes in Oklahoma.

By the early 1960s the policy of termination had again been discredited by protests from both Indians who preferred to remain separate political entities and others who argued that reservation Indians were not ready for complete independence. In the last decade the pendulum has returned, and Indian reservations again are to be supported and developed, but with a major difference — the Indians themselves will be given an increasing role in determining how the aid is to be utilized.

Indian Programs

Though the aims have changed, the pricetag has grown substantially in recent years. In fiscal 1973 the federal government spent about $1.1 billion on Indian programs or $2,000 per reservation Indian. Half of this money was channeled through the BIA and the balance through a variety of other federal agencies.

FEDERAL AID TO INDIAN RESERVATIONS (MILLIONS)

Total	*$1,134*
Educational programs	428
Health	218
Social services and welfare	253
Other	74

• A variety of programs have sought to develop Indian agricultural, forest, and mineral resources and to expand the industrial and commercial base on reservations. Federal agencies manage forest and range lands, negotiate leases, provide legal assistance, and seek to attract business to reservations by providing roads and transportation, housing for workers, industrial parks, tax breaks, credit and contract guarantees, land and buildings, and subsidized wages and training for employees.

Indian lands totaling 52.6 million acres make up the greatest part of personal and tribal Indian wealth. Indian returns from all types of land use are low, both because the lands themselves are unproductive and because Indian and government managements have failed to obtain maximum yields. For example, Indian farmers do more poorly than nonIndians, in part because the best Indian lands are leased to nonIndians but also because Indian farmers lack the capital, knowhow, and in some cases acreage to be efficient. Likewise, mineral leases, in some cases, have provided less than fair returns to Indians. Often the recovery of new mineral and timber resources does not lead to the development of associated on-reservation processing and manufacturing plants.

Business development has been only modestly successful. Before 1961 there were only six companies established in Indian labor force areas. By December 1972 there were 230 plants operating on or near reservations employing 7,460 Indians, with an annual payroll of more than $30 million.

The road to Indian industrial development, however, has not been as smooth as the steadily increasing numbers of plants and workers might indicate. One inevitable problem has been the high rate of attrition of new businesses. Another difficulty has been the limited degree of Indian investment in and ownership of new plants. A third criticism has been the lack of employment opportunities for skilled male workers at the new plants. The new facilities tend to employ semi-skilled laborers and many hire mostly women. Another problem has been the lack of industrial discipline among Indian workers. Turnover and absenteeism have been reported to be high, and productivity low at some plants, particularly during the early months of operations.

• The BIA funds a boarding and day school system which educates about 25 percent of Indian students. In addition, supplemental funds are provided to state and county supported school systems to help to educate the majority of Indian children who attend public schools. The quality of schooling available to Indians has been sharply criticized. Boarding schools have been charged with inadequate care and instruction; public schools have been criticized for diverting federal funds to the education of non-Indian children. In addition, Indian schools have been faulted for failing to employ sufficient numbers of Indian teachers. So far the federal response to these problems has been to appropriate additional money for Indian education and to encourage the establishment and development of Indian schools controlled by the tribes themselves (a dozen of which were in operation by 1973). As yet the success of these efforts is unclear.

• The Indian Health Service, an arm of the Pubilc Health Service, operates 51 hospitals and contracts with a number of other health delivery services to provide free medical care to all reservation Indians. Periodically the IHS has been criticized for insufficient staffing and services, and these reports have sometimes led to bureaucratic reorganizations and stepped-up funding. These cycles of reevaluation, and the recurrent criticism of the lack of professional medical personnel of Indian descent, should not obscure the considerable progress made by the Indian Health Service in improving health standards, sanitation engineering, dental care, and use of medical treatment facilities by Indians.

• Federal agencies also provide a number of other social services for Indians on reservations including welfare, housing aid, police protection, tribal government operation, and land and trust management. All told these services and stipends carried a price tag of about $250 million in fiscal 1974, with welfare payments accounting for about half this.

The problem with all of these services is that they are provided by the federal government. Inevitably such total control of the pursestrings has come into conflict with developing Indian awareness and desires for self-determination. The BIA in recent years has attempted to foster Indian tribal governments and has sought to turn as much policy-making and operational authority as possible over to Indians, but so far this program has made little progress. The federal government is still operating an almost total welfare society on reservations.

"The Indian Question"

Ever since the Indians were placed on reservations, federal officials have been attempting to "solve the Indian problem." But no policy, slogan, or program has succeeded in rectifying the initial mistake of uprooting Indians from their lands and forcing them to live on the most barren, resourceless, unproductive lands which no settlers wanted.

There are still no answers to the "Indian question." Indians themselves are often bitterly divided as to what their status should be since it is clear that the traditional life on reservations is not compatible with the prevailing social and economic values of American society. Several facts, however, stand out:

• The problems of Indians are better termed the problems of reservations. Off the reservation, Indians are better off than other American minorities, though they still suffer by comparison with whites. It is those who elect to remain or are stranded on tribal lands who face the most severe economic, educational, health, and social problems.)

• (Heavy government expenditures have helped to improve conditions on reservations. Indian health care, educational facilities and enrollment, social welfare, and housing on the reservation have been upgraded, though critics would charge that the improvement has not been nearly fast enough.

• (Money alone will not resolve the remaining more difficult problems on reservations. These thorny issues have to do with fundamental cultural differences and with the basic status of Indians on reservations. The economic independence which most planners concede must be a prerequisite to true Indian self-determination, is nowhere in sight. This is not only a problem of lacking resources — human and natural — but also of insufficient technical assistance. Indians whose values were not attuned to competitive capitalist economics were ill-prepared to aggressively pursue success in agriculture, business, or industry even if they had been offered the opportunity. (A century of dependence on the federal government has exacerbated rather than alleviated this problem.)

Whatever steps are taken to ameliorate Indian conditions must reckon with the evident conflict between the rhetoric of self-determination and inevitable reality of federal control of the pursestrings. (The disputes between militants who want total independence and older tribal leaders who fear "termination" represent a basic conflict that cannot be resolved to everyone's satisfaction. Until this basic "Indian question" is resolved, the economic and social problems of Indians on reservations are no more likely to be solved in coming decades than they were in past centuries.

VI

THE MOMENTUM OF CHANGE

Are minorities moving toward equality or are the problems they face more intractable than in the past? Are some
groups advancing much faster than others? The foregoing
review of the changing status of blacks, Mexican-Americans,
Puerto Ricans, and Indians provides few unequivocal
answers. Not only is there a great deal of uncertainty about
basic data relating to population, income, employment, and
educational achievement, but many critical issues remain
unexplored. For example, only speculation is possible about
the scale of illegal immigration, the prevalence of illicit
and unreported income, the extent that female-headed families may have an adult male present unreported to census
takers or welfare workers.

Even the most complete marshalling of information would
not provide indisputable interpretations. Data on absolute
gains may yield one picture, but relative improvements
another. Problems may be serious, but progress may be
encouraging, and emphasis can be placed on either the half-
full or half-empty glass. Normative judgments are involved
in interpreting seemingly objective facts such as the meaning of marital and family pattern changes. Moreover, the
meaning of many past and present developments can only
be known in the future. Nevertheless, the foregoing analyses
highlighted several developments which are unequivocally
documented and which have relatively clear-cut implications.

The Bright Side

• The income of minorities increased substantially over the last decade and a half. Government transfers and increased earnings have reduced measured poverty, while dramatically expanded in-kind aid has ameliorated the associated deprivation even more. A "basic needs level" of health care, housing, and nutrition are now widely available, and the problems associated with the lack of the essentials have been alleviated, though not completely eliminated. On the other hand, there has been, at most, a very slight increase in the ratio of minority to Anglo income. Yet, maintaining a constant or even slightly growing share of a rapidly expanding pie may be viewed as an accomplishment, at least in the sense of measurably improving well-being. Comparatively, it appears that the greatest gains were made by blacks, with smaller advances for Indians, Chicanos, and Puerto Ricans.

• The labor market gains of minorities have been absolute and relative. For males, there was a shift from laboring, frequently agricultural jobs, to the operative and craftsmen categories. There was an exodus of minority women from household and service work into operative and clerical jobs. Increasingly, minority workers have entered the employment mainstream where they are represented by unions, covered by social insurance, and eligible under private welfare plans. More visibly, average earnings have risen dramatically, with minority women catching up to white women of the same age and education, and younger minority males closing the gap somewhat. Less encouraging are the facts that minorities have moved upward to the lowest rungs in each occupational category; the most disadvantaged males have dropped out of the labor force, deceptively improving average status. Relative unemployment rates have not improved, and the gainers in the 1960s were the most vulnerable in the subsequent recessions. Overall, however, the positive labor market developments far outweighed the unfavorable ones. Labor market inequality has been reduced, and the status of minorities improved.

Again the greatest gains, at least between 1960 and 1970, appear to have been made by blacks, followed closely by Indians and Puerto Ricans. Chicanos also improved their occupational status but at considerably slower rates than others.

• Educational gains have been substantial. The younger generations of blacks, Mexican-Americans, Puerto Ricans, and Indians are still less likely than their white peers to finish high school and to enroll in college, but the racial differentials have been dramatically reduced. In this case the greatest strides, measured by proportions of high school graduates, were made by Indians, with blacks, Puerto Ricans, and Chicanos gaining less rapidly. While it is doubtful that the relative rate of achievement per year of attainment has improved for any of these groups, the added years of schooling have meant increased learning and credentials. If this does not insure equality in the labor market, a diploma is an important force pushing in this direction; while the income differentials between high school graduates and dropouts are less for minorities than for whites, there is still a substantial payoff to education.

• Birth rates have declined substantially for all minorities, though the decreases among Indians and Chicanos have not been as great as those among blacks and Puerto Ricans. In all cases the declines have been less than or equal to those of whites, so that all minorities will continue to have greater numbers of dependents than whites in the foreseeable future.

• Minorities have gained a fairer (though still incomplete) measure of their "inalienable" civil rights. Since blacks have suffered most from discrimination, these changes have benefited them most. Equal access to public facilities has been generally established, eliminating the most visible and demeaning injustices which affected all minorities to varying degrees. Employment opportunity has not been equalized, but legal efforts have been increasingly effective and few employers practice the overt discrimination of a decade ago. Disparities in the quality of public education (as judged by expenditures) have been reduced, and de jure segregation has been largely eliminated. Fair housing has been established in principle more than practice, but minority families which are excluded do have legal redress, and some start has been made toward requiring fair housing plans and ending exclusive zoning laws.

• Minority groups are better organized and cognizant of their interests, and minority problems have been placed high on the nation's agenda during the 1960s. "Benign neglect" in the 1970s was in contrast to the general indifference of the 1950s and before. The courts and federal agencies now monitor school integration and educational progress. The Equal Employment Opportunity Commission (EEOC) and the Office of Federal Contract Compliance (OFCC) have a continuing mandate and increasing powers to eliminate labor market discrimination. Minorities have greater access to the press and to the public. Voting rights have been effectively guaranteed, though minorities do not take full advantage of these privileges. Blacks, Mexican-Americans, Puerto Ricans, and Indians have achieved little power, but recognition has been accorded to their problems and institutional forces now support and defend minority interests.

Negative Developments

• White flight from central cities to the suburbs has been

massive, leaving behind blacks, Puerto Ricans, Mexican-
Americans, and urbanized Indians. Minorities remaining
in rural areas or reservations are as isolated as ever.
Areas with concentrated minority and low income populations are
likely to experience increasing difficulties in maintaining
schools and other services as the business tax base departs
in search of greater amenities and as affluent white suburbs
turn their backs on the problems of neighboring jurisdictions with severe problems and diminished resources. The
grim consequences are already evident in some central city
areas as social and economic capital deteriorates while the
exodus of the affluent from all races accelerates.

• The husband-wife family unit has become less prevalent
for some groups. The combination of limited education
and earnings, greater labor market gains for women than for
men, a welfare system that encouraged separation or non-
family formation, and urbanization in general played havoc
with the marital and family patterns of blacks and Puerto
Ricans, though not urban Mexican-Americans and Indians.
The consequences were more female-headed families, increased dependence and low average family incomes. The
subsequent impacts on education, social behavior, and general well-being are debatable, but few would argue that the
changes improve the future prospects of these minorities.

• The "welfare explosion" in the 1960s and 1970s increased dependency among minorities, leaving large segments of the populations living on public assistance and
social security programs. While this has helped to improve
the income of recipients, dependency may also have undermined motivation for upward mobility. The welfare system
also probably contributed to the rise of female-headed families among minorities. Whether the benefits of higher income outweigh the costs of family disruption and reduced
self-sufficiency is open to debate.

• The recession, and perhaps changed national priorities, greatly affected all minority groups. Income and employment gains slowed in the 1970s, and some were reversed. Behind the statistical declines are the frustrations of individuals who worked hard to get better jobs only to lose them because of limited seniority, the dashed hopes of struggling organizations and businesses which foundered as economic conditions deteriorated, and the depressing treadmill of improved living standards gradually eroded by inflation and stagnating opportunities. Even where advances exceeded reversals, the tolls of adjustments to minorities and the rest of society were costly.

Contributing Factors

• Government policies and programs have been of basic importance. Civil rights laws removed many impediments separating minorities from the mainstream, and the courts were fundamental in translating principles into practices. Minorities were disproportionately the beneficiaries of expanded needs-based income transfer and in-kind aid programs. Compensatory education and remedial training, minority enterprise, economic development efforts, and various community action endeavors, have had mixed ratings of effectiveness. But overall, they provided minorities with a "piece of the action," creating jobs, upgrading opportunities, and establishing a base for organization. The federal government's efforts and exhortations were also the impetus for many broader economic and social developments, altering the attitudes and behavior of public institutions and the business sector.

Government action was not always beneficial, however, and some programs have had adverse impacts. As noted, welfare policies apparently contributed to the family deterioration experienced by blacks and Puerto Ricans. The lack of any consistent strictly enforced immigration policy worked to the detriment of Mexican-Americans and also Puerto Ricans. Empasis on Big Brother-knows-best policies robbed reservation Indians of self reliance and nurtured the dependency of the Indian population.

Economic gains come easiest for those at the end of the line when income and employment growth is most rapid. The sustained prosperity of the 1960s was unequivocally a major factor in the absolute and relative improvements of minorities. Conversely, those at the margins are most vulnerable when conditions deteriorate, making the recessions of the 1970s particularly onerous for minorities.

• The geography and composition of growth are also important. The rapid expansion of service and clerical employment in the 1970s generated large numbers of jobs for workers lacking intensive training. The growth of white collar jobs allowed many whites to move into higher status and more desirable positions, opening opportunities for minorities in lower-status, but not necessarily lesser-paying, craft and operative positions. Despite the frequently noted suburbanization of employment, the number of central city jobs per resident increased in the 1960s. Some depressed rural areas also gained as employers seeking unutilized workers created jobs in labor surplus areas.

• The other side of the picture was the substantial movement of minority populations to take advantage of expanding economic opportunities. So much attention has focused on urban ills that the traditional and continuing roles of cities as upgrading mechanisms has been obscured. The migration of black, Chicano and Indian workers from rural to urban areas was a major factor in improving the status of these groups.

New immigration into the United States tended to affect

minorities adversely by increasing the competition for low
level jobs. The status of Mexican-Americans is directly affected by the number of "green carders" and illegal immigrants in the Southwest, just as Puerto Rican gains were
made more difficult by the influx of illegals from the Caribbean.

• Activism of minority groups was a catalyst of change.
The civil rights struggles, mounted first by the blacks but
later by all minority groups, forced the issues of discrimination onto the national agenda. The urban riots, whatever
their negative impacts, pried loose governmental pursestrings
and led to an increase in the scale of efforts. These publi-
cized confrontations were only the most visible tip of an ice-
berg. More crucial to the progress of minorities were the
substantial changes in public attitudes. The widely proclaim-
ed backlash of the "forgotten American" did not reverse
the trends toward increased public acceptance of equal employment opportunity, equal education, and fair housing.
The debate focused on how far, how fast, and by what means
these rights were to be secured, rather than on whether basic
rights were to be guaranteed.

A Range of Interpretations

The debate persists about the meaning and implications
of these major developments. Some argue that the gains of
minorities have been sufficiently pervasive to put them in the
socioeconomic mainstream, and that the American "melting pot" has succeeded once more. Diametrically, some claim
than an underclass has been created for whom welfare, illicit activity, disrupted family structure, and limited work
commitment are a way of life, precluding long-run progress.
A variant is the issue of whether there is a "secondary labor
market" or a new class of minority jobs which perhaps pay

more than the traditional "dirty work" of the past, but are characterized by high turnover, little training, and limited advancement opportunity. The alternative is that minorities have moved up several steps on what is a relatively continuous occupational ladder, and have moved into the internal labor markets of large firms where progress will occur over time.

Another open issue is the isolation of minorities. The ghetto, reservation, or barrio may be viewed as either an area of concentration or an area of confinement. Some analysts feel that the central city is still performing its traditional role as an upward mobility mechanism, with disadvantaged residents improving their education and income, acquiring new cultural traits, and inter-marrying or moving into the suburbs. More pessimistic observers consider the central city a dead end, with minority residents cut off by housing discrimination, limited transportation, and low-quality education, unable to move up to better home environments and jobs. Similarly, some have revived the argument that *de facto* segregation in public education is not critical as long as educational systems are equalized, while others feel that bussing or even stronger measures are required to equalize educational opportunity.

There is also debate whether the gains of minorities will stall in the face of increased opposition. Some feel that the progress of the 1960s did not threaten the rights or privileges of the majority and was, therefore, relatively easy to achieve, whereas further advances will require a "pound of flesh" which the majority will not easily relinquish. The controversy over bussing or employment quotas illustrates this thesis. A more positive view is that the struggles in the early 1970s were symptoms of painful but continuous progress.

A final, crucially important issue is whether blacks, Mexican-Americans, Puerto Ricans, and Indians really share the

same set of identifiable "minority problems." There is some
evidence that Mexican-Americans and Puerto Ricans are
following historical patterns of upward mobility for immigrants, and that their transitional problems will pass in a
few generations (unless a new immigrant flood makes it more
difficult for them to climb the ladder). Indians, on the other
hand, suffer the continuing dilemma of having to sacrifice
some of the special support and cultural independence of
reservations in order to achieve greater economic and social
equality. Off the reservation, Indians tend to improve their
economic status; yet within reservation boundaries the future continues to depend overwhelmingly on federal aid
programs. Black problems are far more persistent and far
more the results of society's racism than of transitional difficulties or personal decisions. Skin color still seems to be
the major factor in discrimination, and blacks are worse off
than brown or "red" minorities. Despite more than a century of emancipation, blacks remain second class citizens,
isolated and oppressed by individual and institutional pre-
judice. While strategies such as compensatory schooling
and aid to attain higher education, income maintenance, birth
control aids, health care, housing, and affirmative action to
guarantee access to jobs may improve the status of all minorities, the problem of racial discrimination will not be
solved without more deep-seated (and therefore long term)
changes.

The Uncertain Future

Each of these areas of uncertainty about the past clouds
the future. Implicit in the "underclass" theory is the predic-
tion that the next generation of minorities — bred into addi-
tudes of dependency, lacking stable family relationships, trapped in secondary labor markets, and isolated in low-income

areas — will be as bad off as the last. If the doors have become harder to open, and the majority more resistant, then progress will be limited. On the other hand, the pay-off on education and training may have been delayed, so that conditions may improve on their own as the better educated age and begin to raise families.

If the above observations are not far off the mark, then the force and direction of the last decade's change remain unpredictable, and there is no crystal ball to predict the future. Given the severity of the current recession, there are reasons for pessimism. It does not follow, however, that seven lean years must follow seven fat ones.

Whether the government will play as central and active a role in the next decade is also unknown. There has been a leveling off in the growth rate of social welfare expenditures, and there is continued debate over reform of the system. If need-based aid is retrenched, minorities will suffer. If, on the other hand, a more comprehensive and compassionate system of guaranteed income is implemented, minorities will benefit disproportionately. The intensity of equal opportunity efforts is also a question mark. The controversies over busing, zoning, employment quotas, and the location of low-income housing may eventually recede. Alternatively, in troubled times vested interest groups may gain adherents in opposing affirmative goals or other changes. The progress of minorities may also be stymied by legislative action if a large majority opposes court decisions implementing antidiscrimination statutes.

Though increasing political representation at all levels, expanding educational attainment, higher income, and increased influence on the media will all add to the political leverage of minorities, the ultimate determinant of future minority progress is the will of the majority. If voters and taxpayers feel that other needs are more pressing, if vested interest groups resist rule changes aimed to help minorities, if individuals perceive themselves threatened by the gains of others, then progress will be difficult.

Clearly, blacks, Mexican-Americans, Puerto Ricans, and Indians remain far behind other Americans by almost every measure of socioeconomic status, despite some evident progress. Recent developments, which in many cases wiped out the relative progress achieved so torturously in the 1960s, are disheartening. The vast gap between minorities and the rest of the nation demonstrates that equality of opportunity, much less equality of status, are still distant goals. Two hundred years after the birth of our nation, we are still struggling to put into practice the Founding Fathers' principle that all people are created equal. The question is whether in our third century an affluent and compassionate majority will be willing to end the injustices and inequalities based on race and color.